Little White

How to Bring the Magic of Angels into Your Life

Katie Golby

Angels descending, bring from above,
Echoes of mercy, whispers of love.
~Fanny J. Crosby

O welcome, pure-eyed Faith, white-handed Hope,
Thou hovering angel, girt with golden wings!
~John Milton, *Comus*

Dedicated to my mum- the most loving, caring and nurturing woman I know. How can I not believe in angels when I was blessed to have one as a mother?

Contents

Introduction

Strange coincidences which you can't explain. Hearing just the right message for you at the right time. Seeing or feeling things that seemingly have no clear logic behind them. For some people these experiences can be written off, explained and dismissed. But, what if there was another reason for these strange occurrences? A truly wondrous and magical reason that touches each and every one of us, whether we realise it or not? What if the seemingly unexplainable was only the attempts of our Divine friends trying to communicate with us, guide us and help us however they can? Dear reader, let me share with you an amazing truth: angels are real! Not only this, but they are attempting to make their presence to all of us every day. This book will help you understand who our angelic friends are, how working with them can bring untold blessings into your life, and help determine the ways in which you can connect with them. We are going to go on a beautiful and life changing journey together that will bring magic and miracles into your life!

My own angel experiences may at first glance appear to be a very slow starter. I was born into a family who had no solid religious beliefs at all. Indeed, my father was an atheist who found the whole notion of spirituality one that he was unable to get on board with, due to his very rational and logical mind. My mother, on the other hand, was always open to spiritual matters and has become more so as we have both gotten older, but as a child the only real spiritual influence in my life was school. Yes, I learnt about Easter and Christmas from a Christian perspective, but aside from saying the Lord's Prayer every day in assembly, I don't recall any kind of real religious or spiritual matters being overly discussed at all during my formative years. My childhood instead seem to centre around dance lessons, reading and eating lots of sweeties; certainly nothing that would hint at the direction my life would take in later years. And yet, even at a young age, I always knew there was something different about me, something that separated me slightly from those around me. You would never know it to look at me, for there was no obvious sign or mark of my inner turmoil, but as the years rolled by these feelings grew. Outside I was an outgoing and friendly girl, but inside I felt hollow; as though there was an aching void that I was unable to fill. I now know that this feeling was my spiritual self which was feeling ignored and isolated, but for years I had no clue why I felt so lost and unfulfilled. Desperately, I tried to make myself happy with an unending merry go round of doomed relationships, unsuitable professions, and hobbies that felt shallow and fake; none of which brought me any closer to the happiness I was looking for. Mind, I may not have been connecting to my angels then, or was even fully aware of their presence, they were continuously trying to make themselves known to me!

Looking back now, it's clear that there were two key times in my life that really stand out for me in regards to my early angelic connections; and they were times that certainly saved my life! The first occurred when I was 20 and pregnant with my first child. It had been a fairly difficult pregnancy: my blood pressure had been up and down and I'd suffered with terrible morning sickness. None of this was helped by the fact I was in an unhealthy relationship with my child's father, and the stress of it all was definitely having a very negative impact on how I was feeling. Around 32 weeks I visited my midwife on the advice of my grandparents who had commented on the swelling in my feet. She admitted that my blood pressure was a little high and that she would come to see me at home in a few days. She never came. On the following Friday I was at home on my own reading, as my partner was at work. The house was peaceful and I was enjoying the quiet, when suddenly I heard a loud and distinct male voice in my right ear: "Go to the doctors now!" Immediately I spun round, expecting some intruder to have broken in unnoticed, but there was no one there; I was completely alone. With thumping heart I wondered whether I had simply imagined the voice, but there was an unshakable feeling deep inside that told me I needed to follow the advice of the disembodied voice and get myself to the doctors. When I got there, the doctor took one look at me and told me to get myself to the hospital straight away. It turned out at I was suffering from pre-eclampsia, and both my life and that of my unborn child were both in real danger unless I had an emergency caesarean straight away. My son Jack was born that day, 7 weeks early and weighing only 3lb 12oz. I never told anyone about what had happened back at home. I was worried that others would think I was crazy and not believe me. So I buried the strange experience deep into my subconscious, until events ten years later dragged them up to the surface. This time I was ready for them and was in a place where I knew they would never be able to be ignored ever again.

Ten years later I was travelling down to Cornwall to see my mum and my step dad with my son, my husband and a family friend. We had recently purchased a second hand car from a local private dealership, and I had become increasingly uneasy with it as the days had gone on. The whole car felt more and more unsafe and unreliable, and I couldn't shake off the creeping anxiety that knotted in my stomach. Still, I was desperate to see my mum, so off we set. Half way on the journey we stopped off for refreshments. Getting back into the car, we set off again and made our way back onto the motorway. Suddenly and without warning, all the electrics in the cars simultaneously cut out and the engine went dead. Fear gripped my heart and silently I screamed "Someone help us, please!" It was a bank holiday Monday and the roads were extremely busy with holiday makers heading off to the coast for a break, and yet the lane we were in was mysteriously clear of traffic. Not only this, but the car rolled onto the hard shoulder and off the carriageway *after* it had stopped. As we pulled out of harm's way and the traffic roared past, we stared at each other open mouthed, unable to believe what had just happened. We should be sitting on the road still, about to be hit by oncoming traffic at any second, and yet we had miraculously been moved out of danger, with no logical explanation as to why.

2010 was a pivotal turning point in my life that started my spiritual awakening and saw me tentatively step onto the path that would ultimately see me connecting and communicating with the angels on a daily basis. Events in that year allowed me to evaluate my life and to fully comprehend that life is too short to be miserable. You should spend your valuable time doing things that make you joyful, give you fulfilment, and to always aim to be true to who you really are. It was then that I also came across the inspirational author Doreen Virtue, whose books helped me to identify who I really was and why I was here. Suddenly my spiritual being shot into the fore in bright and wonderful technicolour, bringing with it immense feelings of fulfilment and joy. From that moment on I absorbed everything I could about various spiritual fields: tarot; psychic ability; auras; past lives; meditation; and a whole other range of differing information. But, the one I kept coming back to time and time again was the field of angels. Initially I was resistant to the angelic realms. I was worried about what others would think of me and the links to Christianity that I was keen to move away from. However, the angels clearly had other ideas for me, because they kept drawing me back in. And the more I learned about them, the greater sense of complete comprehension, peace and fulfilment I felt. The final piece of the jigsaw came when I was given my own psychic reading, where I was told in no uncertain times that my life purpose was to work with the angels and to help introduce other people to their love and guidance; a truly blessed life purpose.

That's what this book is all about. Whether you are new to the whole field of angels and have picked up this book out of sheer curiosity. Or maybe you are becoming increasingly concerned and worried about the events happening round the globe, and are looking for spirituality to bring you the uplifting guidance you are seeking. Perhaps you even know about angels already but are looking to expand your knowledge and connect with them on a deeper level. Whatever your reason, this book will introduce you to the magical world of the angels, and will help you to connect with them so can you bring their love, miracles and guidance into your life. Together we will see that the angels are always there for each and every one of us, no matter who you are. Let's take those first steps down the path of angelic love together, and welcome the blessings into your life!

Throughout the book there is sections of text in blue. These are direct messages to you which I have channelled from the angels. May you find them as loving, enlightening and inspiring as I do xxx

Chapter One

What Are Angels?

The word angel derives from the Greek word 'angelos', which means messenger. Angels are Divine beings who act as a link between God and humanity, bringing forth messages of love and peace to all. Not only this, but these celestial beings are here to guide, protect and to help each and every person to be more happy and at peace. Angels are pure beings of light who have no specific gender or race, but who do tend to appear to people in the form that each individual feels comfortable with. Each one of us has our very own guardian angel who stays by our side from the moment we are born right through life until we die. There are literally millions of angels that can be called upon to help you with any problems you may find yourself dealing with, but our guardian angel is like our best friend. They know us better than anyone; will work with us to try to achieve our life purpose; and will always love us unconditionally. Angels see our inner spirit and know that, although human behaviours and actions can be deemed as being negative or wrong, that inside we are pure love. Angels do not judge us for the things that we do, but they will always try to help us for our highest and greatest good.

"You are so loved. More than you could ever realise. You seek people and items outside of yourself to make you feel happy and whole inside, but there really is no need for you to do so. You are already whole- complete in mind, body and spirit. We have been with you since the beginning of your journey, and we will always be with you. We are your constant companions, and our love for you is never-ending."

As well as our guardian angels and the millions of angels that are always available to help us, there are also the Archangels. These Divine beings oversee all of the angels and all humanity, and each one has a particular role to which they can provide us with guidance and help. The Archangels will be covered in more detail later on in the book, but know that these powerful beings are also available to us all whenever we need help or guidance. The angels are here to help bring peace, love and harmony to the world, and they know that they can do this by working with each individual at a time. Some people worry that their problems aren't big enough and that by asking for angelic assistance they may be taking up an angel's valuable time when the angel could be of more use to someone else. As I have already mentioned however, there are literally millions of angels all waiting to be called on for help. Not only this, but the Archangels are omnipresent, as they are all part of the Almighty, so can help countless people at the same time. Never worry that your problems are not big enough to ask for help. The angels know that stress can take happiness and peace out of your heart, so will always help whenever they are asked to.

"The modern world is such a dark and stressful place to live in. We know you have come here at this time for a specific reason, and you will each contribute in pushing the Earth forward into its next stage of growth and spiritual evolution. We do know how tough life can be, but know that if you make mistakes that is part of the journey. You are here to learn and grow, and nothing you could do could ever take our love away from you. We always see the pure light of your soul, and nothing can diminish that for us."

Welcoming angels into your life is a truly positive experience that can bring you many blessings. Angels can help us physically by such things as saving people's lives and healing the sick; mentally by bringing inspiration and solutions to problems; emotionally by giving strength and courage, and healing wounded hearts; and spiritually by helping you determine your life's purpose and to lead a more spiritual life. And there's countless more worries and concerns that they can bring guidance and help for if you ask them to. Angels can help with issues concerning children, career, money, family- the list is endless! They are here to help with all aspects of human life and can bring balance and joy to each area of our lives.

You may have noticed that there is a key component that keeps coming up when I talk about working with the angels: you have to ask the angels for help if you want them to. Humans are born with free will and no angels can intervene in a person's life unless you ask them to; no matter how much they want to. It is therefore paramount that you always call for angelic help when you feel you are in need of it. It does not matter how you do this and you do not have to be down on your knees in prayer for them to listen to you. You can use any words that you feel comfortable with, and you can say the words in your mind, aloud or even write them down. The words you use are not as important as the intention behind them, and this is what the angels are actually responding to. All that matters is that you *do* ask, and the angels will come to your side to help in a flash!

So, now that you know what the angels are and how welcoming them into your life can help you, let's look at how we can do this. The first step is to understand that angels are sending us signs all the time. These signs are to let us know that they are with us, as well as giving us the guidance which we are seeking. Signs are numerous, as we will discover in the next chapter.

Chapter Two

Notice the Signs

The angels are continuously sending us signs. As well as letting us know that they are with us, they also act as confirmation of a decision you have to make; if it is the right thing for you to do in line with your highest and greatest good. The problem comes of course that a lot of people are not recognising the signs they are getting, or are dismissive of the ones they do notice. And yet, once you are aware of the angel's 'calling cards' you will begin to notice more and more of them in your everyday life, which can lead to a wonderful sense of comfort and the guidance which you have been searching for. The most important aspect in all of this is faith: if you believe something is a sign, then it is. Do not allow your logical mind to quickly dismiss a miraculous moment. Signs tend to be repetitive in nature also, and will normally coincide with questions or prayers that you have communicated to the angels or to God.

"We send you countless signs that we are with you every day! We are here to offer you our love, guidance and support as you move along your path, and we long to let you know that you are not alone. Keep your eyes open for the messages we send you and feel the love radiating out from our spirit to yours."

The angels know you extremely well, and so will know which sign to send to you to grab your attention and to create a truly meaningful moment for you. When you notice one of the signs listed below, thank your angels for reaching out to you with love and guidance. So, what are the common signs from the angels which you may come across?

Feathers

One of the most well-known signs from the angels is finding feathers, especially when they are in unusual places or they seemingly appear out of nowhere. Feathers are directly linked to the prayer, question or thought that has been dominating your mind, and you will always tend to know what the feather is related to for you. Although the most well-known of these is the white feather, which conjures up lovely images of fluffy angel wings, the angels do leave other colours relevant to the message they are trying to send you:

- **White**: this is a sign from the angels to let you know that they are with you. Spirituality, faith, protection, purification and hope

- **Black**: this feather typically appears when you are going through a time of crisis, and it lets you know that the angels are aware of what you are going through and are here to support you. Protection, repelling or warning of negative energy, mystical wisdom, you are undergoing a spiritual initiation, growth or increased wisdom
- Yellow: a lovely congratulatory message from the angels, and a sign that everything is going well right now. Mental awareness, joy, cheerfulness, intelligence
- Pink: the angels are joining in the joyful and happy feelings around you right now, and want to share these positive feelings with you. Unconditional love, romance, caring, compassion, harmony, faithfulness, honour, inspiration
- Blue: the angels are asking you to find a space of peace and calm- whether in meditation or out in nature. Peace, inspiration, spirit connection, psychic awareness
- Red: this colour is always linked to matters of the heart, and show that the angels are helping to bring love and passion into your life. Good fortune, passion, emotions, courage, money, security
- Green: a very healing colour, this shows the angels are sending you the healing you need. You can help with this by taking good care of every aspect of your health. Health, healing, nature, money, prosperity, success, nature/plant/animal spirits

- **Grey**: a message to be patient whilst everything seems quiet, and to have faith that the angels are helping you behind the scenes. Continue to follow angelic guidance, and know that everything will come to you when the time is right. Peace and neutrality
- **Orange**: carry messages of creativity, listening to your inner voice, and staying positive to attract success. Energy, change, optimism, success, new ideas, physical love
- **Purple**: messages of deep spirituality, transmutation of negativity, as well as the opening of psychic and spiritual sight. Universal consciousness, spiritual connection, heightened spiritual growth
- **Brown**: signify grounding, home life, and stability. There is an energy of respect, grounded positivity, and balance between the physical and spiritual. Endurance, home, friendship and respect

I have had numerous experiences in finding feathers, and they always fill me with feelings of love and blessings. As I mentioned, it's even more magical when you find them where you'd least expect. Like setting up my twin's highchairs two days in a row, and both times finding white feathers on the seats! There's no way these feathers could've come from an external source. I knew the angels were showing me that they not only walked with me, but they were also guiding and supporting my children. It was truly a magical find.

Coins

There's an old saying which I was continuously told as a child, "see a penny, pick it up, all day long you'll have good luck." Even before the knowledge that the angels leave money for us a sign, I understood that finding coins was considered to be a good luck symbol. But it does go a lot deeper than this. Angels can leave money for you to find in unusual places, and can also make it appear out of thin air! I have found coins in beds, on bookcases and in the sink; all where I was 100% certain they had not been previously.

Every aspect of the money you find has meaning for you: the place you found it, the time of day, the amount, the material of the currency, and any messages upon it. Angels can leave us coins and higher amounts in paper form, but when you find one out of the blue know that it has been purposefully placed there for you to find by your angels. Finding any form of money makes us feel supported-financially, spiritually and emotionally.

Clouds

Look closely at the picture above. You may see the distinct shape of an angel in profile, with his wing arching into the sky. Angels can provide signs of their presence and guidance by changing the shape of the clouds above our heads, and it's always so magical when it happens! Clouds themselves are heavenly bodies of moisture that watch over us from above, and they are a common angelic sign because they can be formed and shaped to create any image the angels wish to portray to you. As well as angel forms, I have also seen clouds shaped like feathers, wings and even a heart.

Butterflies

Butterflies are such delicate creatures that remind us of the natural cycles of life, along with the transformative nature of it. They show us that by welcoming change into our lives we can make the whole process easier on ourselves rather than fighting against it. Butterflies are also a symbol of rebirth, and can remind us that when we think all hope is lost and we've hit rock bottom that is when we can actually grow upwards into something truly beautiful.

So, when a butterfly comes to you, especially if they flutter close and will quietly rest by your side, know that it is a lovely angelic sign. Butterflies have traditionally been seen as spirit travellers, and the way in which angels can travel from the higher realms to ours. They may come to you when you feel you are experiencing a setback, or are going through a big period of change and transformation. Butterflies can also be a message to take a break and stop working so hard. If one comes to see you when you've been sitting at your computer for long periods, know that it's time to get outside for a rest.

Birds

The presence of birds, especially in excessive number or if they behave unusually can be a sign of angelic presence with you. As mentioned, one of the most well-known signs is feathers, and the birds definitely have an abundance of them! For years I kept have situations with our feathered friends were I felt under attack: I was chased by a swan, a goose and I have had a pigeon land on my head (stop laughing!) Because of this I was steadily building a phobia where I was convinced that every bird I saw was going to attack me in some way. However, when I started to connect with the angels on a deeper level I suddenly found that birds were coming to me more and more. But rather than behaving in an aggressive manner, they would sit and simply look at me. Robins have walked up to my feet with their heads cocked to the side and looked me deep in the eyes, and starlings have congregated in vast numbers in my garden where before we only had pigeons! It's been a gradual process, and they certainly haven't pressed their presence on me too hard, but bit by bit they have come closer to me. And thankfully, my growing fears have since abated too.

Rainbows

We are all familiar with the Biblical tale of Noah and the ark, and the rainbow that came after the floods. Rainbows are a truly beautiful sign that show us Divine love, protection, support and care. If you pray or ask the angels a question and then see a rainbow, you can be assured that the whole situation is under the loving care of the angels. It's also possible to see double rainbows, albino ones (where you see the shape but not the colour), and even moonbows (rainbows that appear at night from moonlight)! These three occurrences are rarer, so we can be in no doubt of the messages of love and support that the angels seek to convey to us. I had my own special rainbow experience when I was feeling particularly low one day. I asked my angels to send me a sign to show me that they were with me. That day was a very hot and dry one, but as a stepped outside there was one little cloud above me, and upon it was a lovely little rainbow! My spirits instantly lifted and I felt so much comfort knowing that my prayers had been answered.

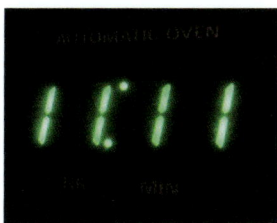

Numbers

Seeing repeated number sequences are a clear angelic sign that can give us clear guidance, once we are able to find out the meaning of each number. You may feel drawn to look at the clock or a phone number, only to see that the same numbers are showing themselves to you each time you do. Or a car may drive past you with a registration pate that has a particular relevant number sequence for you. Spiritual writer Doreen Virtue has produced a book that helps you to interpret what these recurring number sequences mean for you, called Angel Numbers (Hay House, 2005). However, I have listed the basic meanings of the numbers 0-9 for you here:

0 this shows that you are one with the Divine, and to feel this love within you. It also indicates that a situation you're in has gone full circle

1 this number indicates that your thoughts are rapidly manifesting into reality for you, so the angels ask you to keep your thoughts as positive as you can so you don't get something you don't want! The Universe has taken a photograph of your thoughts and is now working to give you what you want.

2 your hopes and dreams are coming to fruition, so make sure you keep nurturing them. Don't give up on your wishes just before the miracle happens! Everything is manifesting as it should. Keep positive, keep affirming and visualising, and it'll soon be yours!

3 the Ascended Masters (such as Jesus, Buddha, Moses, Mother Mary and Ganesh) are with you, giving you their love and help. Call on them for guidance and you will receive it

4 you are surrounded by angels! They are with you to give you the love and guidance you seek. Don't let worries dominate your mind because the angels are giving you the help you need

5 big life changes are headed your way! These changes are not necessarily 'good' or 'bad', but are part of the natural flow of life. These changes are in answer to your prayers, so keep positive and go with the flow

6 your thoughts are out of balance and are too focused on your material needs. This over focus means you have stepped away from you spiritual nature and you life's purpose. Be rest assured that when you focus on how you can be of service to others, your material needs will naturally be met

7 the angels are sending you so much praise! You are on the right path, keep up the good work you're doing, and know that blessings are headed your way. A really positive sign of miracles coming

8 a part of your life is coming to an end, and this shows you to be ready for it. Rest assured there is light at the end of the tunnel for you, and make sure that you harvest the fruits of your labour along the way

9 a number of completion, this shows that you have come to the end of a big phase in your life. It also asks you to send you love and healing to the planet, both in prayer and in action, as the Earth is in desperate need of care

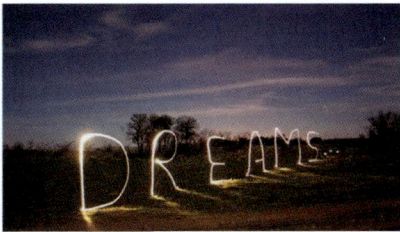

Dreams

Angels can give us the guidance we seek within our dreams. They can appear to us themselves, or they can send us dreams that answer our questions. When having an angelic led dream you will find that an external disturbance will happen to suddenly wake you up. This typically happens right when you're in the middle of the dream, and you may be very annoyed to be taken out of the lovely dream you were having. Rest assured, this is deliberate, and happens so that the angels can be certain of you remembering your dream when your mind is fully conscious. You can train you mind to recall your dreams yourself too by keeping a dream journal by your bed. As soon as you wake up write down everything you can remember, even if it makes no sense. At first this may not be very much, but if you keep doing it you are telling your mind that you want to remember your dreams, and you'll find that you are able to recall more and more.

One of the most vivid dreams I had concerned a horse! I was outside a shop waiting to go in, and the most beautiful golden horse was brought out to me. As I ran my fingers over her silky hair, I was told that she was a gift for me and she was mine to keep. Immediately I woke up, and I checked in with my intuition and angels as to what the dream meant. It turned out the angels have given me a golden horse as my new animal spirit guide. I felt so blessed, especially when I started to look up what it all means online. Horses symbolise such qualities as travel, power, freedom, wisdom, spirit and change. Having a horse as a spirit animal is to help you on the new adventures and changes that are starting to dominate your life. It reminds us to keep moving ahead in our lives and reaching for our goals. The horse totem wants to awaken you and help you find your true self, and your true desires. Horses being power, courage, and energy to those who seek it. Horses are given to people who are friendly, adventurous, compassionate, willing and free spirited. The fact that the horse is gold is symbolic too. Gold is the colour of wealth and endurance. Gold is symbolic of empires and kingdoms. It has the energy of the Sun, of confidence and courage. I thanked the angels for this miraculous gift, and have worked with my spirit animal to welcome all changes in my life.

Sparkles of light

The angels can make you aware of their presence by allowing you to see sparkles or flashes of light with your physical eyes, as well as orbs. These lights may be seen out of the corner of your eye, as your peripheral vision allows you to see more things that have supernatural origins then if you look at them straight on, or you may see them via a camera. These sparkles are a physical manifestation of angelic movement, like the trails of a lighted firework. Whether flashes of light, sparkles or in orb form, seeing these light forms are very special indeed. Most are white in colour, though it's possible to see variations in the hue of them too. Different colours link in to the Archangels, more of which in later chapters.

Reading or hearing something

Angels have often been known to send messages through music, and everywhere they travel to they are typically accompanied by some sort of music; whether in the environment or through clairvoyance. If you continuously hear the same song, or songs with a similar message, ensure that you pay attention to the words of the music and the message contained within it. The title of the piece can also be a clear message to you in relation to your problems or concerns. Angel signs can also become apparent through overheard conversations that seem to give you the answers and guidance you've been seeking, or someone coming to talk to you out of the blue who says just the thing you needed to hear. You may even be thinking of someone and suddenly receive a telephone call or message from them!

Signs can also be given through the things we read. Flicking through a magazine can give us a phrase or article that gives us the guidance we've been worrying about. Whilst I've been in book shops and libraries, books have literally fallen off the shelves in front of me that have given me invaluable messages of hope and help! Try this: pick up a book, ask your angels a question, and then flick to a random page; don't be surprised if there are words of encouragement or answers to your problems.

Even billboards can be used by the angels to give you the right guidance at the right time. When my mother in law was diagnosed with cancer and was extremely poorly, I was extremely worried about her. The next day, whilst in the car, we drove past a new billboard in my home town with the words 'Live Life!' emblazoned upon it in large letters. I knew it was a sign from my angels to make the most of everyday because you never know when things may change and you won't be able to anymore. It certainly gave me a new appreciation for my health, my family and my life.

Feelings

The final common sign that the angels are with you is simply a feeling that they are! This can happen as feeling a gentle brush against your skin; goose bumps on your skin when it isn't cold; a sudden temperature change in the air; hearing your name being called when there's no one there; feeling as though you're wrapped up in soft wings; and having a sudden overwhelming feeling of love without any obvious source. An inner knowing that comes from our higher selves knows when an angel is nearby, even when your rational mind tries to dismiss the natural feelings that are occurring inside. If you feel as though you're not alone then the chances are the angels are with you.

Now that I have listed the types of signs the angels leave for you as confirmation of their presence and guidance for you, hopefully you'll have a heightened awareness of them and will be spotting them in your everyday life. If you're looking with no success, try the following:

Angels,

Please give me a clear sign, which I'll easily understand, that you are with me giving me support, love and guidance

Thank you in advance for this blessing

And so it is!

All you need do then is to be aware of things around you. The sign may not come immediately, but rest assured, within 24 hours you will receive an angelic sign. As mentioned previously, aim not to let your rational mind dismiss things out of hand too quickly, or you may miss something beautiful. Also, try not to look too hard for a sign. When you do this, you emit an energy of desperation, which in turn means that you don't really believe that the angels are going to send you a sign, or that you are worthy enough to receive one. Having a negative mind-set like this can actually block your connection to the angels and stop the signs coming through so easily for you. So, by all means be aware of the things happening around you, but don't desperately look for signs every second of the day. They will come to you, normally as confirmation of questions or prayers that you have asked the angels to help you with. Have fun and enjoy the blessings that come your way!

Chapter Three

Different Types of Angelic Connection

For a long time there seems to have been a belief within society that only a few special people had psychic ability: to be able to see the future or make connections with those beings in higher realms. And yet, this isn't the case. In actual fact each and every individual upon the Earth has the ability to be psychic in some way. Before you dismiss this was a scoffing laugh, let me explain.

Modern society as we know it has set up and is consistently reaffirming the notion of the separateness of life. Through consumerism, materialism, competition and the corporate world, we are continuously bombarded with messages that separate us from one another. We may have the feeling that we are better than others because we perceive we have more than them, and can therefore look down our noses on those who we judge as being 'less' than us in some way. By the same token, we may feel that other people in the world are somehow better than us because we have the belief that they have more than we do and this makes them 'more' than we are. These feelings of separation ultimately lead to feeling of being alone in the world, being misunderstood and judged. At the extreme end it is also for the basis for acts of violence, segregation, discrimination and war. Believing that we are different from those around us makes it difficult for feelings of love and compassion to fully flourish in the human race, as well as bringing a plethora of problems.

And yet, these feeling of being separate from one another are completely false. God is within all of us, and we are within Him. It is said that human beings are the Divine experiencing life in all of its forms; that we are God in solid, human form. Therefore, we are all one, like waves in the ocean rolling to the shore but still being part of the collected body of water. Each and every person upon the planet shares the same collective energy. There is no separateness, no division, and no differences on a spirit level. To fully understand the true nature of oneness you can then see how if one person is able to fully utilise certain skills, then these skills are available to all of us. If a person can run a four minute mile, then we all have the ability to do the same. And if someone has psychic abilities, then we all do.

"How we wish you would see that you are all part of the Great Spirit. There is no division between you and the person sitting next to you; you are all the same. The oneness of life extends to every living organism that inhabits the Earth, and there are no boundaries between you and everything else. When you hurt someone else, you are only hurting yourself. When you extend love and kindness to all, you are also giving it to yourself. Do not then seek to act out your anger or hurts on others, for it serves you no purpose. Instead, let the love pour from your

heart out onto the world, for it is only through this action that the world and you can truly know peace."

I liken psychic ability to a door inside our minds. Some people's door are wide open and the abilities are able to be fully utilised to help others. Some people's doors are closed but unlocked, and the person can develop their skills whenever the desire to do so arises in them. Other people's doors are not only closed, they are locked. These people have no interest or belief in psychic ability and will never be able to engage with the natural skills that are within them. The point is, we all have a door whether it's open, closed or locked. We all have natural psychic ability in our beings, whether you realise it or not. With practice, patience and belief all of us can work on engaging with and developing these skills.

You may be aware that there are differences in the abilities that those who are engaging with their abilities seem to have. Stories abound of people seeing angels standing bold in front of them, but others may have more success in hearing the angel's messages of love and guidance. There is a collective word for psychic sensitivity that incorporates the different senses: clair senses. Clair means clear, and each one of us will have all the various abilities within us, though one will tend to dominate over the others. In this sense, it links to the current understandings within the field of education- that each student has a preferred learning style; whether auditory, visionary or kinaesthetic. In terms of the psychic senses, the different types are clairvoyance, clairaudience, clairtangency, clairscent, and clairsentience. What do these words actually mean?

- Clairvoyance: This means clear vision or clear seeing. Someone who has this preference is able to perceive things within their mind's eye that may not be able to be identified by others. The things that are seen are not bound by the normal limitations of time or space.

- Clairaudience: Using this ability means the person is able to perceive things using their outer and inner ears. In this sense, it could be seen that the person is hearing voices or music that may not be heard by others.

- Clairtangency: This means clear touching. It is more commonly known as psychometry. It is the ability to handle an object and perceive psychic information from the spiritual or ethereal realms using touch. Clairempathy means 'clear emotion'. It is the ability to psychically tune into others emotions. Someone with this ability tunes into the vibrations of the spiritual and ethereal realms and feels the tones of another's aura.

- Clairscent: Is seen as clear smelling. It is the ability to perceive a fragrance or odour through psychic senses. Someone with this ability can perceive odours that is not of a physical nature. It is the ability to perceive the essence of a substance from the spiritual or ethereal realms using smell

- Clairsentience: This means "clear feeling" and relates to the sense of touch. It is the ability to perceive energy fields through physical sensations using psychic senses. This includes auras, vibrations, and the presence of entities. When you get a "gut feeling" about something, you are using your clairsentience. What you're doing is using your second chakra, the sacral chakra, to sense things on an emotional level. Clairsentience can pick up what other people are feeling. Clairsentience often works with another ability called precognition. Precognition is the ability to know what is going to happen in advance.

So, are you interested to see what your dominant clair may be? Take the quiz below to give you a clue about it. The answer may surprise you!

<u>Quiz: What Clair Do You Have?</u>

1. Think of a flower, what do you imagine?

A) The hard stems contrasting with the soft petals

B) A lovely flower garden

C) The intoxicating fragrance

D) Hearing the rustle of the wind through the flowers

E) Making potpourri

2. If I say the word 'chocolate', what's your initial response?

A) You can feel the chocolate oozing as it deliciously melts in your mouth

B) You see the label of your favourite bar

C) You can practically smell those cocoa beans zooming up your nose!

D) You hear the sound of the bar as you snap it in two, followed by the crunch as you take your first bite

E) "The diet starts tomorrow!"

3. You are walking along a tropical beach at sunrise. What is your attention drawn to the most?

A) The sand tickling between your toes

B) The sun peeking its head above the horizon

C) The salty freshness of the ocean air

D) The sound of the waves as they crash along the shoreline, and the cry of the birds overhead

E) You search for your camera to capture the moment for you

4. You are in a market and find yourself in front of a stall selling all kinds of items. You want the perfect thing to

help you develop your psychic abilities, what do you choose?

A) A beautiful crystal- you can feel the energy pulsing through your hands

B) A deck of tarot cards

C) A bundle of sage used for smudging

D) A CD of spiritual music to help you meditate

E) A journal to record your dreams in

5. Imagine your best friend is sitting next to you. What do you find easiest to visualise?

A) The feeling of their skin against yours as they give you a cuddle

B) The colour of their eyes

C) The smell of their perfume or cologne

D) The sound of their voice

E) The things you would talk about

Mostly A's: Clairtangency. You are certainly led by your sense of touch, both from external sources and those that seem to come from more spiritual places. This is also known as psychometry: you can handle an object and pick up on details about the person it belongs to. You are extremely sensitive as a person. You may pick up on temperature changes or feel an angel's touch when they are with you. You will talk about how things make you feel, rather than what you think about them.

Mostly B's: Clairvoyant. You are able to see things in your mentally using your third eye (the energy centre located in between your psychical eyes). You are able to see things that are beyond the realms of the things that the majority of us can naturally see with our eyes. Pay attention to your dreams, as they can provide you with a wonderful way of connecting with the angels. Also look out for angelic lights, and things you may see in your mind's eye during meditation (more on this later).

Mostly C's: Clairscent. You are very led by your sense of smell, and have a very sensitive nose for the smells in your environment. However, your abilities go deeper than this, for you can actually 'sniff out' the facts about things when there may be no obvious clue or reason why you feel this way. You may pick up on smells or fragrances when there's no clear source of their origin. Angels can sometimes leave the fragrance of flowers when they connect with us, and you'll certainly be aware of it.

Mostly D's: Clairaudient. You are able to hear sounds or voices that may not have their origins on the Earthly plane. You may hear angelic music whenever you are connecting to the angels that plays within your mind. Or you may hear the angels calling or even talking to you!

Mostly E's: Clairsentient. You are the type of person who just seems to know things, and the hunches you receive from your intuition tend to be extremely accurate. You pick up on signs and the angelic presence using your whole body, and can sense when an angel is with you even if there is no obvious sign that they are. It's almost as if you're picking up on the higher vibration of the angel.

Once you have identified which method you will have the most success with, you can start to fully work with it to connect with the angelic realms. There are 20 key ways that you can connect with the angels, these are:

1. **Ask and invite**- you have to invite the angels to help you, as they abide by the law of free will. Write your intentions on a beautiful card and place it somewhere high and light. You could say, *"Angels, I welcome you into my life and I give you permission to guide me, support and heal me in any way that links to my highest and greatest good."*

2. **Pray for help**- a simple of gratitude of requesting help in your life will be responded to by the angels

3. **Crystals**- go to a shop or market stall where crystals are being sold. Ask the angels to help you choose a crystal that will help you to connect with them, then hold your hand out above the stones. Slowly move your hand over the different variety that is available there. When you feel a clear sign on a particular crystal you will know that this is the stone for you to work with; tingling, feeling of heat or an inner knowing that it's the right one for you.

4. **Angel altar**- make a loving space and attend to it regularly with crystals, candles, angel statues, flowers, incense, and anything else that makes you

feel connected to the angels (more of this in chapter 6)

5. **A familiar space of love**- relax in your favourite in nature and surrender. Let go of all the stress you have been carrying around with you, and then open your heart to guidance

6. **Meditation**- this is a wonderful way of connecting to the celestial realm, and is fully covered in chapter 7

7. **Wishes and dreams**- give yourself three wishes every day; whatever your heart truly desires. If you want your dreams to come true you have to make sure you know what those dreams are!

8. **Visualise**- ask your angels to show themselves to you, and imagine your dream, wish or desire. Truly feel, taste, know that it will manifest for you.

9. **Chant**- when you repeat a rhythmic phrase in a melodic tone, it allows the sacred message held within the music to radiate through you

10. **Affirmations**- focus on an intention and repeat it regularly as an affirmation or command to the angels. For example, you could say *"I am a successful and financially independent person"* or *"I am open to love in all its forms"*.

11. **Make a decree**- when you have a specific and important request, send out a stronger plea to the angels by creating an angel decree stating your demands in a loving manner

12. **Write a letter**- communicating with the angels can be done through writing in a journal, diary or a blog. The more creative the better!

13. **Music**- this is a wonderful way to carry messages to the angels. Use angelic songs of love to sing for the dreams you hold, as well as to share any sorrow within your soul

14. **Arts and crafts**- surround yourself with beautiful objects and images as offerings to the angels. These can be bought or even made yourself

15. **Walk in nature**- Take a long walk in nature. Really immerse yourself in the experience by feeling the grass beneath your feet, touch the trees and paddle in the cool water. Feel your connection with the angelic realm through the wonder of the nature around you.

16. **Dancing**- losing yourself in music and letting the beat move your body is another great way to connect. It can be any kind of music, but know the joy that flows through you as you dance will also connect you to the love of the angels

17. **Water**- fill a bath with sea salt, some rose quartz crystals and essences you feel drawn to cleanse you and clear any negativity from your body. Talk to the angels as you bathe, and share your hopes and fears with them

18. **Sacred places**- Visit the numerous amount of sacred monuments and ancient stone circles that are dotted around the world, including many in this country. These spiritual places are very often surrounded by angelic beings who will happily help you

19. **New moon**- holding a ceremony personal to you during a new moon can help you focus on fresh starts, new beginnings, ideas and projects; especially

those related to feminine energy. This can be done simply by writing your pledges, desires or thoughts on paper, then burning the paper outside in a safe area. The smoke from the burnt paper will draw your intentions out into the angelic realm. Ask the angels to help you with this process if you feel drawn to it.

20. **Full moon**- the full moon is all about completion, so you can ask the angels to help bring forth any issues to a gentle and loving conclusion for you.

Fears and Blocks

As I have discussed, connecting with the angels is open to everyone, regardless of their age, gender, race, religion, or any other determining factor. The angels do not judge as the human race does, and are here to help anyone who calls upon them. Their mission is to bring peace and happiness to all, so that is always their determining factor, so long as it is in line with each individual's highest and greatest good. Despite this fact there will be those who will struggle to connect with the angelic realms and other beings who inhabit the higher realms. This can be for a variety of reasons:

★ Considering it blasphemous to talk to the angels- within some organised religions it is believed that you should only pray to God, Jesus or some other high spiritual being. Thus, trying to connect to the angels may cause a sense of fear and block your spiritual development. However, the word angel means 'Messengers of God'. They are gifts from the Divine Creator, carrying messages between us and God, as well as bringing us the guidance we need. Sacred texts, including the Bible, are filled with stories from people who benefited from angelic help, and this has continued right up to the present day.

★ Panicking that they won't receive any messages or help- many people really push to make things happen because they worry they won't be able to hear their angels, or even worse that they don't have any angels with them at all. Remember that we all have angels with us all the time, whether we believe in them or not. But having this anxious fear as your base emotion will only block anything happening. God and the angels will come to you when you open up and are ready. Rather than push too hard and worry, enjoy the process and go with the flow! You'll soon find the signs cropping up all over the place

★ Worrying that you're just making it all up- messages from the angelic realms are always full of warmth, love and compassion; without compromise. The angels are here to help us be happy, so they will always try to make every situation of your life better for you; whether this be your relationships, career or health. True Divine guidance will repeat itself until the message gets through and you make the changes you need to make. These repetitions can differ in that they may come as thoughts, then through feelings, then through visual signs for example, but they will keep coming until you take the action you need to take. Any thoughts that come once and don't repeat, tend not to be angelic in nature. So just wait if you are unsure and see if the message comes again for you. Also be aware that any message from your ego will try to belittle you and make you feel as though you are not worthy to talk to the angels, or go for your dreams. Know that these messages are not from the angels at all, but from your ego. Angelic messages are always filled with love, ones from your ego tend not to be. Angel's messages always talk to 'you' and 'we', whereas the ego will always focus on 'I'. If you do hear any negative messages that worry you, ask Archangel Michael to protect you and remove any lower energies and entities away from you.

★ Thinking they are supposed to work things out for themselves- a lot of people think that life is all about suffering and working through challenges on your own so that you can learn and grow. Yes, it is true that we can grow this way, but we will develop faster through love and peace. The latter also inspires those around you to move towards love too, so it is for the good of everyone. Know that the angels won't do everything for you though. Sometimes miracles do happen, but they are more likely to give you the Divine guidance you need to help yourself.

The angels don't want us to live our lives in fear, for it is a toxic energy that contaminates everything and everyone it touches. Fear will hold you back from living a fulfilled and happy life. Fear will have a negative impact on your health. Fear causes wars, greed, abuse and suffering on all levels. But if you open your heart and mind, and choose to see things differently, you may see that there is a better way to move through life. Moving away from fear and into love in all of you words, thoughts and actions will ultimately prove healing for you and the world. The angels can help you to do this and bring truly wonderful blessings into your life, if you let them. Let yourself be open to the wonders of these celestial beings and you will soon find your life lit up brighter than the Sun itself.

"Fear closes your mind and your heart, not only to the angels but the whole world around you! You speak of loving your fellow man, but how can you when you're so fearful of him? Moving down the path of fear will only bring you unhappiness, stress and misery. When you turn your thoughts away from fear to love, you allow the sunshine of all creation to enter into your being and lighten you up from the inside out. Only then will you truly be able to love one another, and bring the healing to this planet that is so desperately needed. Whenever you find yourself slipping back to the old grey fog of fear, choose another thought. Choose love instead."

Hopefully the different methods listed above will have given you some inspiration for making your own angelic connections. But, first, let's take a minute to familiarise ourselves with the angels that are all around us so we know who we are connecting with.

Chapter Four

Nice to Meet You!

There are so many angels waiting and eager to help you! Within this chapter I will introduce you to them and explain how calling for help from specific ones can bring the relevant blessings and guidance into your life. The different religious dogmas found around the world may differ in their opinions of the angel's names and roles, but I am going to introduce you to three main types of angels, as these are the ones you will typically be working with. That's not to say there aren't others in the higher realms, but they don't tend to have the same level of interaction with us as these do. So, what are the three types of angel that you will come into contact with?

1) Guardian Angels

Every single person upon the Earth has a guardian angel! Whether you believe in angels or not, or whether you think you deserve to have one or not, is completely irrelevant. All of us are blessed to have this angel by our side from the second we are born until we pass back into the higher realms. In fact, because your guardian angel knows your life's purpose and the lessons you have agreed to focus on whilst you are here, they will stay with you throughout every incarnation you have! They are bound to your spirit, not just your Earthly body, and will continue with you throughout your many lifetimes; guiding and supporting you every step of the way. For we are all spiritual beings having a human experience, as opposed to merely human beings striving to find a spiritual experience. Spirit is the core essence of who we are, and our purpose is to learn the lessons we need in order to grow and develop. Our guardian angel is here to assist us with our own personal mission, and they will do whatever they can in order to help us on our way. They love us unconditionally no matter what we do, and will always try to lovingly steer us onto the right path. They have a high vibrational energy and have never lived any lifetimes themselves upon the Earth.

"Your guardian angel is your life long companion. They know you better than anyone, even better than you know yourself, and they love you more than anyone else ever could. To them you are the most perfect and amazing being that has ever lived, and it is their duty to help and guide you however they are able to. Know that you are never alone in the big world, for a winged friend is always by your side."

2) Angels

As previously mentioned, there are literally millions of angels and they are all willing and eager to help you! Angels are pure beings of light who were created through God's thoughts of love for us all. Whenever you need any kind of comfort, assistance, guidance or protection, you can call upon the angels for help and they will gladly do everything they can. They are especially happy when they see someone who has the intention of wanting to bring more happiness and healing into the world, in whatever way is most suitable to their own skills and talents, and they will give help in these endeavours. Because there are so many angels available to you, you can ask them to surround you, your loved ones, your home, your business and your vehicles. You can ask for as many angels as you like in line with your own needs. Remember to occasionally say "Thank you" for the help they give you. This isn't so much for their benefit, but for your own. Be thankful and grateful opens up your heart to love, and brings more blessings into your life.

3) Archangels

These are extremely powerful angels who oversee all the angels and guardian angels that are present upon the Earth. In this sense they could be viewed as having an arching view over all creation, or taking up a managerial role within the angelic realms. Each archangel has a specific role which they specialise in, and for which you can call upon them for help. Like all angels, the archangels are pure beings of light and have no specific gender or race. However, because of their own speciality, each archangel tends to be viewed as being either masculine or feminine in accordance with the role in which they guide us. Having specific names and supposed genders means that we feel more connected to them as human beings, and so makes it easier for the angels to help us. There are many archangels, and different religions will tend to focus on a certain number, but I will introduce you to each of them and explain their role so that you have an understanding of them all.

Archangel Michael

"Life is a challenge for all human beings who walk upon the face of the earth. Darkness looms up and can threaten to overwhelm you at any given opportunity. It can be so tempting to cower in the shadows or to allow yourself to give in to the fears that hide in plain sight. But there is another way; a path towards the Light. Working with me and all of the angels can ensure that you discover and are able to fully harness your own inner light, and shine it so brightly that you the dark has no choice but to vanish. Life is difficult, but I am always here to stand strong by your side, giving you the courage and focus to walk the path of love of truth. Do not allow fear to get a grip on you in any way, for darkness only truly enters when it is invited it. Stay strong and true, and always let your light shine."

Michael's name means 'He who is like God', and he is probably the most well-known of all the archangels. He is traditionally known as a warrior angel because of his alignment with the virtues of strength, courage and protection. Indeed, within many modern works of art he is typically portrayed with a sword hanging by his side, or holding it high into the air. This is not a sword as we know it however, heavy and made of metal, but it created from pure light and is ready to destroy the fears we each hold within our minds so that we can move forward towards true peace and happiness. Michael is the great protector, whether of our own lives, our loved ones, belongings or vehicles. There have been countless stories of his intervention to help save people's lives (including my own miraculous tales at the beginning of this book). You can call upon Michael's protection whenever you start a journey in any type of vehicle, be it by road, water or air. He will always ensure your safety whilst on the move. If you find yourself travelling and you've forgotten at the start to ask for help, you can still call upon him for instant support should a crisis of any kind occur. Trust that if you are concerned or feeling stressed about the safety of your belongings or loved ones, that Michael will help you by keeping a protective eye over them all. He, like all angels, is omnipresent, so you are not diverting his attention by asking for help with this or any other matter.

Not only can Michael protect objects and people, he can also offer spiritual protection. Fear is the primary force that can take away your sense of peace it it's allowed to get a grip on you. Michael can help to shield your from any lower negative energies that may pull you into fear if you ask him to do so, and if you follow any intuitive guidance or warnings he may provide for you. Michael can help to shield you from any kind of spiritual or psychic attack where someone who is angry or jealous is sending you negative energy, either consciously or unconsciously. He can also clear away any negative energy that has come your way already, and the impacts of it upon you. Calling on Archangel Michael can give you the courage to face any situation that may be intimidating you, whether it be examinations, presentations or surgery. The innate strength of this great archangel will naturally pass to you should you ask for his help.

An energy field is emitted by each archangel that can be described as a halo of light around them. Each form of energy has a different vibration rate which gives it its own unique colour. For Archangel Michael his halo can be seen as either being a rich purple or a royal blue in tone. It's possible to sometimes see flashes of these colours when he is near you, along with a noticeable rise in temperature in the air around you, which comes from the light of his ever present sword.

Associations:

Colours- royal purple, gold and royal blue

Crystal- sugilite

Astrological sign- oversees them all

Scents- sage, rosemary, frankincense and chamomile

Planet- The Sun

Element- Fire

Direction- South

Season- Summer

Day- Sunday

Flower- Marigold

<u>Archangel Raphael</u>

"You are whole in the eyes of the Lord; complete in every way. Human bodies are prone to illness and disease, which in turn takes away the happiness from your mind. I will help restore you to complete and full health so that you may move forward in peace and harmony. Health is

everything. When your health suffers you cannot function fully or happily in any other area of your life. Call on me to help you, but help yourself too. See your body as a beautiful temple that houses your spirit. Look after the sacred site and keep it functioning well. Only then can you truly access the divine part of yourself: your divine right to be whole, happy and at peace."

Raphael's name means 'God heals', and he has a long tradition of being known as the angel for all matters related to health and healing. It is thought that we are actually all whole and healthy in the eyes of God, and Raphael's job is to reveal the true nature of this for our rational, conscious mind. As already mentioned, all angels require our permission so that they can help us, even though they may be incredibly keen to give us the guidance and support which we need. Archangel Raphael is no different in this manner, and you will find that when you ask him to provide healing for yourself or another that the effects are almost instantaneous.

Not only can Raphael give you the healing which you need himself, but he is also able to guide people to receive the healing they need from a suitable practitioner. He can relieve any pain you may be experiencing due to either chronic illness or short term conditions. Animals too are not seen as being unworthy of appropriate healing from Archangel Raphael. Whether suffering from injury or illness, Raphael will bring much needed healing to any animal in need. Clearly the animal is unable to ask for help for themselves directly, and all angels fully understand this. Any person who is concerned for an animal's health and wellbeing can ask for help on the animal's behalf, and the help will be given in the same way.

In the same tone, you can ask Archangel Raphael to bring healing to someone else. If the other person is willing for the healing to be given then it will be. However, because of the undeniable fact that we are all born with free will, if the person does not want to be healed for whatever reason, then Raphael has to honour this choice. He will stay close to them though, which will bring said person both blessings and love. The only exception to this rule is if the person for whom you want to send healing is not fully conscious, if they're in a coma for example. In this case it's impossible to ask the person if they would like some angelic help with their healing, but both you and Raphael can ask the permission of the person's higher self to see if the healing can take place. If the healing isn't wanted then the healing won't be able accepted in. In any case, this kind of healing won't cause the unconscious person any harm, so you can still ask on their behalf.

If you yourself feel that a career within the healing field, either in Western medicine or more alternative methods, is your calling, then Archangel Raphael can help you to make your dreams a reality. If you are unsure which area you would naturally excel in within this field, ask him to help you decide. Be on the lookout then for signs that will guide you in the right direction, whether they are in books, overheard conversations or television programmes! Upon asking Raphael to help you with your career in the field of healing, you will soon come to see that he can help you with any aspect of it. Whether it be financial, education, setting up a business, or bringing in clients: Raphael will assist you in any way you ask him to. Not only this, but when conducting any kind of healing, asking him for help can lead you to truly beneficial guidance for yourself and the client. This will be given to you through your intuition and natural psychic abilities, and can truly create a magical healing environment.

The vibrational energy of Raphael is green in colour, and people will typically see green flashes when they are connecting with him.

Associations:

Colours- green

Crystal- emerald, malachite

Astrological sign- oversees them all

Scents- lavender, lily of the valley, mint, bergamot and thyme

Planet- Mercury

Element- Air

Direction- East

Season- Spring

Day- Wednesday

Flower- Iris

Archangel Gabriel

"Each one you is upon the Earth for a divine and unique reason; and some of you have the most profound messages to share with the world. Now more than ever is a delicate time. The world is in a real state of flux and transformation where multiple possible futures are available to you all. The world needs messengers who will stand up and speak words of truth and love so that the future of the world will be one of peace and happiness. Do not be afraid to speak your message loud and clear, for you were given that message by God to share with all

mankind. I will help you to get your message out to all those who need to hear it in the clearest and most profound way possible. Do not allow your message of hope to sit in the confines of your mind, for it will not be of any use to anyone there. Let me help you share every word, and lift the vibrations of the world to a high and wonderful place."

The name Gabriel means 'the strength of God' and his areas of expertise are those involving children and all those who work as messengers. She is the angel who helps to guide all matters involving children: including contraception, pregnancy, birth, adoption, and raising children. Calling on her help with any of these matters will ensure that they run smoothly, and that everything happens in line with your highest and greatest good. Alongside this, Gabriel can also help those who wish to dedicate their professional lives to working with children. If you wish to guide, support and encourage children to be the best they can be, then Gabriel will definitely help you to make these desires real. Whether it be training, finding a suitable position, or even setting up your own business, Gabriel can help provide all the material requirements you will require.

Gabriel is also the archangel you call upon if your role concerns being a messenger to others: whether it be teacher, writer, actor, artist or counsellor. She is typically portrayed holding a large copper trumpet, and if you have a message to give to the world, Gabriel will certainly help you shout it loud and clear! She acts like a lovingly yet determined motivator, who will keep you focused on polishing your message and getting it in a state ready to share with others. Once it's completed, Gabriel can then help you to share this message with others, and will give you a loving nudge if you're feeling unsure of yourself.

Gabriel's colour is copper, the same as her trumpet. Seeing flashes of this colour, or even finding yourself being drawn to the metal is a clear sign that she wants to work with you.

Associations:

Colours- copper

Crystal- copper

Astrological sign- Cancer

Scents- jasmine, rose, eucalyptus and myrrh

Planet- Moon

Element- Water

Direction- West

Season- Autumn

Day- Monday

Flower- Lily

Archangel Uriel

"Your mind is like the greatest computer you ever could imagine. The information that you have stored in there is unimaginable. However, when you allow fear based thoughts to cloud your mind, the access you have to all of this profound knowledge is hindered. Suddenly you can't do everything you want to do, or be everything you are capable of being. When you call on me to help you I will simply lift the fog of fear away from your mind and allow you to access the information you need in a comfortable

and calm manner. If there is something you need which you are having trouble accessing, fear not, for I will softly whisper the words down upon you in the most loving way. Everything you need in life is available to you. You have access to it all. Do not let your fears and doubts stop you believing this."

Uriel's name means 'the light of God', and he is the archangel to call upon for all matters related to knowledge and ideas. He's a wonderful angel to come to the aid of students, business people, or anyone who is looking for a solution! Asking him for help can ensure that you are feeling more prepared and ready for a test or exam you have to take. When you are in need of answers or ideas, you'll find that he will softly whisper the right ones in your ear, which you will perceive as sudden flashes of inspiration that have seemingly come from nowhere. The vibrational energy of Uriel is perceived as yellow.

Associations:

Colours- yellow

Crystal- amber

Astrological sign- Aquarius

Scents- sandalwood, ginger and basil

Planet- Uranus

Element- Fire

Direction- North

Season- Summer

Day- Tuesday

Flower- Gentian

<u>Archangel Chamuel</u>

"So many people wonder why they are here: what is the purpose of their life. They worry about having enough abundance in their life in all aspects, but they never stop to

actually consider the truth of the situation. You came to Earth for a reason: to learn the lessons you needed to grow in spirit. Your life purpose is aligned to this; it's the soul reason you are here. The other part of the process is happiness, and peace. Life was never meant to be a trial or difficult. No beloved, you are meant to be happy. I will help you find your true life's purpose and give you the guidance you need to start walking down the path of truth for you so that you may know true happiness and fulfilment."

Chamuel's name means 'he who sees God', and because of his omniscient status and clear vision, he is the archangel to call upon when you need to find anything you are looking for. Whether it's a missing object, or needing to find something you feel is missing in your life, Chamuel can see the location and solution of everything that is deemed lost and shine his light on it for you. It doesn't matter how small the item is, if its loss is causing you anxiety or stress, then Chamuel will be more than happy to help you. All angels have the role of helping to reduce stress in human lives so that we may easily find peace and happiness, and finding lost items can help to make this happen. As he can see everything that is upon the Earth, he will have no problem finding things for you!

By the same token, if something is aligned to your highest and greatest good, then Chamuel can help bring it into your life. Whether it be a new job, relationship, home, or anything else that is in line with God's divine plan for you, then he can help bring it to you once you ask him. Once you have asked for Chamuel's assistance in finding whatever it is you are seeking, ensure that you pay close attention to any thoughts, visions and feelings that may come to you, as he will show you the location in this way. Even if you have already turned the house upside down and inside out looking for it, and you're certain that you've explored every nook and cranny, follow the guidance you are given about its location, for Chamuel may have placed the object there after you have asked for his help. His vibrational energy is pale green in colour.

Associations:

Colours- pale green

Crystal- flourite

Astrological sign- Taurus

Scents- mint, geranium, neroli and ginger

Planet- Mars

Element- Air

Direction- South

Season- Winter

Day- Tuesday

Flower- Hyacinth

Archangel Ariel

"What the world needs know is love: love from each and every living soul on the planet. When we exude that love out into the environment, the whole vibrational energy changes and lifts higher. The world is in real need of healing and help, but it's only through a shift in attitude that these changes can become reality. Love every single living thing, for you only have one planet and you need to look after it."

Ariel's name means 'the lion or lioness of God', and she is known as being both the nature angel and the environmental angel. If you feel called to work in any area that is focused on protecting the world's ecology, animals, air quality or oceans, the Ariel is the archangel to ask for help. Archangel Ariel has a real love for all nature and wants everyone to take responsibility for the planet and all its inhabitants. When you hold the same love in your heart for the environment as she does, you will find that she will draw close to you and have a guiding hand in all your work.

She can also help you to connect with nature yourself in a truly lovely and safe way. So if you wish to go camping or hiking for example, calling on Ariel beforehand can ensure that your expeditions are happy ones! Ariel also works closely with Archangel Raphael to bring healing, but her focus on the animals, birds and fish of this world. If you are trying to help an injured or sick animal, Ariel can ensure that your healing abilities get a very angelic boost. It's not only the animals that you can physically see that Ariel can help you with however, she can also draw the nonphysical side of nature to you too if you ask her. Whether it be fairies or other elementals, Ariel can guide you gently and lovingly to making connections with the spiritual beings that populate our natural world. Ariel's energetic vibration is pale pink in colour.

Associations:

Colours- pale pink

Crystal- rose quartz

Astrological sign- Aries

Scents- Jasmine, sandalwood, frankincense

Planet- Saturn

Element- Air

Direction- North

Season- Summer

Day- Friday

Flower- Carnation, delphinium, honeysuckle

Archangel Metatron

"Children of the world are the planet's most valuable commodity, and really need to be treated as such. The vibration of the planet is rising at an accelerated rate now, and the children who are being born and more sensitive than any other generation previously. Do not be so quick to medicate your children and numb down this sensitivity, for it is a gift. The children have been born with this increased awareness for a reason; to help the healing and ascension of Earth. Support them in discovering and developing who they are as people. Being spiritually aware at this time is a difficult process, as they will go up against many people who are closed off to their divine self. They will need your love and encouragement to fully embrace who they are, and to fulfil their vital life's work."

There are two archangels whose names do not end with the –el suffix; Metatron and Sandalphon. The reason for this difference is because both beings with originally human prophets who were rewarded with ascension into the realm of the archangels after death, due to the benevolent nature of their lifetimes. Metatron's speciality is to help highly sensitive children, and those who seek to support and guide them on Earth. Children who are extremely sensitive and have open access to their spiritual gifts are typically misunderstood by many adults within modern society. Indeed, they may even be medicated due to parents and doctors misdiagnosing them as having autism or Attention Deficit Hyperactivity Disorder (ADHD). Metatron can also assist those children who may be having trouble starting and settling in to new schools or homes.

For anyone who feels drawn to helping highly sensitive children themselves professionally, then Metatron can support and guide you to make successful choices along the path. Whether it be training, acquiring a position, or setting up your own business, if you feel drawn to helping children then Metatron can support you. The colour of his energetic vibration is violet and dark green.

Associations:

Colours- violet and green

Crystal- watermelon tourmaline

Astrological sign- Virgo

Planet- Pluto

Element- Fire

Direction- Centre

Day- Sunday

Archangel Sandalphon

"The whole of creation vibrates to a musical pattern that is inaudible to the human ear. There is a rich tone to the Universe and all of life responds to the musicality that resides within every cell of their being. Whether you realise it or not, you are a musical being. Connecting with me will help you to understand this part of your being and to express it in the most beautiful way to share with all

around you. Not all of you are destined to be professional musicians, but you are all innately musical. You come from a creative force, and this creativity winds its way through your core. Allow me to help give it a voice."

Sandalphon's name means 'brother', and he is known as being the angel of music; he may even be the master musician. Whatever form of music a person is involved in, whether playing an instrument, singing or composing, Sandalphon can really benefit those who express their musical abilities. He can help people who are creating songs with magical ideas; help with learning new pieces; or calm your anxieties that may rise up when being asked to play in front of others. We are all children of a creative God, and hold a creative force within us; whether we realise it or not. Archangel Sandalphon can help to express this divine part of your nature, and in doing so can help you to express your own divine nature. His energetic vibrations is turquoise in colour.

Associations:

Colours- turquoise

Crystal- turquoise

Astrological sign- Pisces

Planet- Jupiter

Element- Earth

Direction- Centre

Day- Thursday

Flower- Carnation, lily, ivy

Archangel Azrael

"So many of you hold so much unfounded fear of death because it is the world of the unknown to you. History has countless teachings of Hell and being punished for sins, and yet nothing could be further from the truth. The transition from life to death is not one to be feared, and you will never be held in disapproval or anger for the things you perceive to have done wrong. The only person who can judge you is yourself, and yet in the eyes of God you are already forgiven. You are whole, perfect and loved so strongly that is beyond any comprehension whilst on

earth. Death is another part of your journey, and I will be here to guide you through every step. You will never be alone in the journey of the soul."

Azrael's name means 'whom God helps', and is known as the Angel of Death. This does not mean he is akin to some Hollywood version of the Grim Reaper. Instead he is rather like a loving guide who counsels spirits that have just crossed into the spirit realm after their passing, as well as consoling those family and friends that have been left behind on Earth and are grieving. Any situation that holds feeling of loss, transition and death will see Azrael waiting to help you. He can also give you the support and healing you need in dealing with any feelings of grief.

As well as providing loving support directly, Azrael will also give help and support to those who work as grief counsellors. If you work within this profession, Azrael can help make the energy of your practice benevolent and loving, so that you can fully support those who are hurting and overcome with grief. This also carries on to those who may be called to write or speak a eulogy at a funeral. Calling on Archangel Azrael will ensure that your words will be the most loving and gentle that you could possibly say. This Archangel will guide us all through the transitions of life into death, and his vibration is a creamy white colour.

Associations:

Colours- creamy white

Crystal- yellow calcite

Astrological sign- Capricorn

Planet- Mars

Day- Tuesday

Archangel Jophiel

"Life is not supposed to be a punishment, life is meant to be adored, treasured and loved. Beauty is all around you,

the wonder of nature is a truly breath-taking example of the power of God. You can bring this sense of beauty into your own life with my help. Do not feel that this request is too trivial or menial. When the outside world is beautiful, the inside house of the soul is at peace. Bringing beauty into your life is good for your sense of wellbeing, happiness and self-worth. Call on me whenever you feel drawn to bringing this gift into your life, and I will be more than happy to help in whatever way I can."

Jophiel's name means 'beauty of God', and she is definitely considered to be the angel of beauty. Calling on her for help can bring beauty to every area of your life, including your thoughts, feelings, home, workplace, and within your personal self. In this sense, Archangel Jophiel can help you to become more positive, to focus more on the love and gratitude within your life, and to ensure that you make self-care a priority in every area of your life. If you have any disagreements or misunderstandings with the people you come into contact with, Jophiel can bring her loving beauty to the relationship to heal the problems that may have flared up. She can also bring beauty to your physical self, giving you guidance with all aspects of hair, wardrobe and makeup. These things may seem trivial or too small to bother a powerful archangel with, but the angels are here to bring peace and happiness into everyone's life. They understand that reducing stress and anxiety can help make this happen, so are more than happy to assist with any area that is concerning you; even your physical appearance. Your living and working environments can also be made more beautiful by calling upon Jophiel to help you, and you will find that you may feel drawn to decorating, decluttering and donating your unwanted belongings to charity when you ask her for help. Her vibrational energy is a deep fuchsia, so if you see flashes of this colour, or feel drawn to this hue, you may find this beautiful archangel is waiting to help you.

Associations:

Colours- dark pink

Crystal- rubellite or deep pink tourmaline

Astrological sign- Libra

Scents- Lavender, orange, myrrh

Planet- Mercury

Element- Air

Day- Wednesday

Archangel Haniel

"Within you is the divine spirit of the goddess waiting to claim her natural place in the world. For so long you have suppressed her and held her back, as though the feminine part of your nature was something to be feared. To be whole as a person you need to accept every part of you. Masculine energy has been dominant for so long, and it has helped you build empires and technology that is awe inspiring, but the world is unbalanced. The problems of the world have their root in this lack of balance in the

masculine and feminine energies, and by calling on me I can help you nurture and love your femininity so that it can take its rightful place within the world. Only by doing this can the fear of the planet and the consequential destruction be halted in its tracks."

Haniel's name means 'the grace of God', and she is the archangel who relates to all aspects of women's health issues, both emotional and psychical; who can help you to develop your clairvoyance and intuition; and is the angel of the moon. In this respect she is very like a goddess to those who connect with her, as well as being a powerful archangel. Calling on her for help during a full moon can help you to release anything that you feel has been inadvertently holding you back, as well as healing you in every way. You can call upon her for guidance and support whenever you feel in need of it however, and her loving presence will give you the help you need.

If you are looking to tune into or develop your innate spiritual abilities, then Haniel is the archangel to ask for help. She is the angelic representation of intuition, and you will find the process a lot easier and smoother should you call on her. Although Haniel is the angel that links to women's issues, men can call on her too. We all have a balance of male and female energies within us, and so Haniel can bring this feminine healing and support to everyone. Her energetic vibration is a very pale blue, just like the moon. The gem moonstone can be worn to bring you closer to Haniel, as well as naturally increasing your intuition.

Associations:

Colours- pale blue

Crystal- moonstone

Astrological sign- overseers of all

Planet- Venus

Element- Water

Direction- West

Day- Friday

Archangel Raziel

There are mysteries of the Universe that are greater than you could fathom. God is the most powerful and creative force, and he weaves his miracles throughout all creation. Your spirit journey is a part of this process, for you are a vital part of the whole great scheme of things. Allow me to help you unlock the doors to the secrets that are available to you all. By understanding the macrocosm you will gain a greater understanding of the microcosm. By understanding the Universe you gain greater clarity of yourself."

Raziel's name means 'the secrets of God', and his area is esoteric wisdom. He is akin to an old wizard who is able to shed light onto the mysteries of the Universe so that you receive a deeper comprehension of the wonder of life. His energetic vibration is seen as a rainbow, like light pouring through a quartz crystal. It is said the Archangel Raziel incredibly close to God himself and is able to hear all of the secrets and wisdom from the Creator, which he records in a book. As such, Raziel has access to everyone's Akashic Record: a record of all of life's history. Within this is everything that has ever been done, said and thought; and everything that ever will be. It also documents the contract you made before birth about what lessons you would focus on during your lifetime, and all past lives you have gone through. Working with Raziel helps you to get a better understanding of all of the lessons which you have accumulated over previous lifetimes, and to use this knowledge to benefit your life now. If you have experienced any trauma in your past lives that is having a negative impact on you now, then he can help you to heal it so that you can move forward from a better position. You may also have made vows in previous lifetimes that may be holding you back from achieving true happiness and peace now; whether chastity, poverty or self-sacrifice. Working with Raziel can help to release you from them.

Associations:

Colours- rainbow

Crystal- clear quartz

Astrological sign- Leo

Planet- Neptune

Element- Air

Day- Saturday

Archangel Raguel

"Every relationship that you experience in your life is a teacher. Through these partnerships with others, regardless of the form they take, you gain a better understanding of yourself. Working with me you can ensure that all of these relationships are more balanced, and that you enter each one with love as your focus. Let love be your guide, and let love direct every action. Know that when others lash out at you with their own anger and pain, it is because they are hurting themselves. I can show you that love is the answer for everyone, no matter how they may react to you. Love everyone, and ensure that you

always love yourself, for you are all children of God and you all deserve pure and true love.”

Raguel's name means 'friend of God', and he is the angel who will help to make all of your relationships happy and harmonious. Where there may have been misunderstandings and cross words, Raguel can heal the situation and bring feelings of peace and forgiveness to all involved. If you are looking for new friendships or relationships to enter your life, calling on Raguel can bring people to you who will have the right level of integrity and respect.

It doesn't matter what kind of relationship you are having problems with: romantic, friendship, business or family- Raguel can bring healing and harmony to all. Calling on may bring instant and miraculous healing, but it's possible that he will give you guidance about the steps you can take yourself. This will take the form of signs, feelings and thoughts that keep on repeating, as Raguel will be keen for you to pay attention to the message he's giving you! Raguel's energetic vibration is pale blue in colour.

Associations:

Colours- pale blue

Crystal- aquamarine

Astrological sign- Sagittarius

Archangel Jeremiel

"The past is a valuable tool for understanding who you are and where you want to go moving forward. Fears rise up when people find themselves stuck in the events of the past and unable to move away from the things that have happened. Reflection is invaluable for understanding the journey you are on, but do not allow the events of the past grip you and hold you down. What is important is this present moment, for that is all there is, and you have a choice about how each moment of your life will play out. I

will help you to move forward with crystal clear clarity so that the path ahead is for your highest good."

Jeremiel's name means 'mercy of God', and he is the angel to call on when you are looking to consciously review your life; both on Earth and in the spirit realm. For all souls that have recently departed their body, it is said that Jeremiel is the angel who helps each one review the lifetime they have just experienced before they ascend to Heaven. However, he can also help people who are still here as well. If you are looking to see the events of your life up to this point, as well as where your future is headed for you, then Jeremiel can assist you with this reflection and review. Through his loving heart, Jeremiel can gently guide and mentor us through making any changes for our future in accordance with problem areas that we have identified for ourselves through a life review. His energetic vibration is a dark purple.

Associations:

Colours- dark purple

Crystal- amethyst

Astrological sign- Scorpio

Archangel Zadkiel

"When people have wronged you in some way, why do you hold onto the pain of it? It is not wrong to be upset by the actions of others, but it does not help you to allow this pain to dwell in the seat of your soul. Forgiveness is one of the most important gifts you can give to yourself, for it frees you and allows the light of the Divine to move freely through you. When you hang on to a past hurt you block yourself from receiving the love and guidance that is so readily available to you. Forgiveness is not so much about the person who has caused you so much grief. It's about you and your own sense of peace. Allow yourself to have the harmony that you so richly deserve."

Zadkiel's name means 'the righteousness of God', and is viewed as being the angel of memory. Due to this, he is a wonderful angel for anyone who needs to remember any facts or figures; including students. Working in tangent with Archangel Uriel, Zadkiel can provide wonderful support for anyone who needs to take any kind of test or examination, making you feel better prepared and more able.

Zadkiel can also bring healing to any painful memories you may be holding onto that are causing you pain. Working with him can release you from old hurt and anger, so that you are in a better position to move forward positively on your life path. Calling on him can also shift your focus away from those events in your past that have hurt you to ones that make you feel uplifted, and in doing so will raise your vibration. His energetic vibration is a deep indigo blue.

Associations:

Colours- deep indigo blue

Crystal- lapis lazuli

Astrological sign- Gemini

Scents- sandalwood, ylang ylang, rosemary

Planet- Jupiter

Element- Air

Day- Thursday

Flower- violet

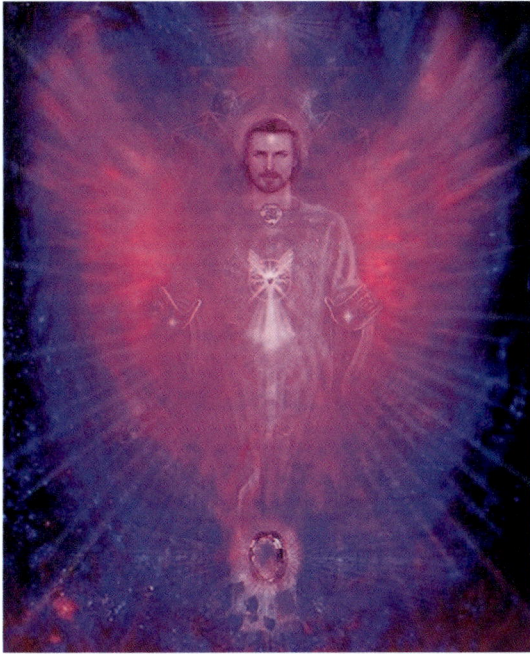

Now you have an understanding of the various types of angels who are all available to connect with, along with the specialities that each one focuses on. Hopefully you've been noticing more angelic signs in your everyday life, but now you're ready to start communicating with the angels in a more definite way. Everything in the Universe vibrates at different energetic rates; and angels are no exception. All angelic beings have very high energy, so if you wish to connect and communicate with them then you need to start the process by focusing on increasing your own vibration.

Chapter Five

Raising Your Vibrations

Every single day we all make choices, decisions that have a powerful impact on us. Not only do these affect our emotional, mental and physical wellbeing, they also play their part on our spiritual self too. Each and every situation, person we meet, action we participate in: they all impact on our energy levels and overall state of wellbeing. All choices can move us to either lower or increase our energetic vibration; whether we realise it or not. Your energetic vibration is something that is in constant flux, always increasing and decreasing, but when you're aware of the things that help you to give you a higher vibration then you can make conscious choices about the things that you do.

When you feel that your energy reserves have been drained and you're vibrating at a low level, then this has a really negative impact on your overall health; including the spiritual part of your being. Having low vibrations can cause you to feel lethargic, be in a negative mind-set, lower your immune system, and even lead to depression. None of us wishes to experience these things in life, instead we long for a life of increased happiness, health and feeling of peace. So, how do we do this? The answer is simple:

Raise your vibration!

If you wish to connect with the angels, and even have the chance to communicate with them, then raising your vibrations is an essential step in the process. Without this, the angels can talk all they wish but you won't be able to hear them as well. It's like tuning your radio into your favourite station: it's easier to get the signal if you have your antennae raised. Increasing your vibrations not only gives you a better chance at this angelic encounter, but also brings a number of other blessings into your life. These include greater feelings of joy, confidence, love, and connection with others. Being able to increase your energetic vibrations means that you can also receive greater abundance in your life, for you attract the things you focus on. When your vibrations are low and you're feeling flat, then your thoughts will be in line with this. Consequently, you will find that the opportunities and situations that come your way also have these same negative feelings attached to them. When you raise your vibration, the positive emotions will bring more wonderful and happy situations to you; and who doesn't want that in their life?

"We have wings to symbolise the lightness of our spirits, and the higher realms within which we inhabit. If you wish to develop your angelic connection then you need to lighten your own spirit, lest your vibration be too dense

and heavy. The process is something that doesn't call for elaborate practices, and if you commit to it you will find that your ability to communicate to us will be unleashed. We are waiting to speak with you, and know that working to raise your own vibration is something that will ultimately bring you untold happiness and tranquillity."

There are a number of things that you can do on a regular basis to keep your vibrations at a high level, so that you can better connect with the angels and bring many more blessings into your life. These are:

★ Appreciate the beauty around you- whether it's a glorious sunset, the smile of a child, or a fragrant bouquet of flowers: taking the time to really notice and appreciate the beauty that's all around you is a wonderful way to raise your energy. It calms the stress in your mind by placing you in the present moment rather than worrying what has been or will be, and it opens your heart to love.

★ Keep a gratitude journal- this is a form of cognitive behavioural training. You form new path ways in the brain that in turn make you more positive overall by consciously looking for the things you are thankful every single day and making a note of them. Not only this, but being able to go back and read your lists at a later date, reaffirms this positive mind-set all over again.

★ Mediate- meditation is a powerful tool that allows you to increase your awareness of self, and to gain greater control over your mind so that you can consciously choose more positive thoughts that serve you, rather than being a slave to whatever your mind wishes to think. Meditation also allows you to increase your spiritual awareness, and in turn will make it easier for you to connect with the angels. Meditation is seen as being something that's really hard by a lot of people, but it really is very straightforward. Make a conscious effort to spend at least three minutes every day to quieten you mind and focus on the stillness inside. You can do this by keeping your attention on your breath, and if you find your attention wandering to other things, to bring it back to this breath. If this proves to be too difficult, then there are many guided meditations available online. Plug in your headphones, make sure you won't be distracted, and follow the words that are being played to you.

★ Doing something for someone else- giving to others is a great way to shift your thoughts from "I don't have enough", to "I have more than enough to give to others in need". Abundance is a wonderful way to increase your vibration, and ensuring your thoughts match this really helps.

★ Listening to music- listening to any kind of music that you really love is really powerful. It puts a smile on your face and raises the frequency of your vibrations. Plus you may even feel the need to break out a dance move or two!

★ Stop complaining and gossiping about others- when we find ourselves repeatedly moaning or participating in being negative about others, we are actually lowering our vibrations. Ceasing this negative chatter, including in the things you read like gossip magazines, ensures that you will start to raise your vibration. Find positive things to say about yourself and others, and always focus on what you're thankful for rather than what you're not.

★ Get up and move- it doesn't matter what form of exercise you take, they all release endorphins into the brain, which is a chemical that promotes positivity and wellbeing. When you feel happier, you will naturally draw happier experiences to you because of the fact that you are now vibrating at a different frequency then when you don't exercise.

★ Hug someone- having a really good cuddle with another person can dramatically reduce feelings of stress, which in turn will help to increase your vibration. Go and give someone a big squishy cuddle!

★ Breathe- when we're stressed we don't breathe properly. Our chests get tight and our breaths become shallow, which in turn makes us more stressed. When you consciously focus on the breath it will naturally start to become deeper and slower. This not only allows more oxygen to enter the body, but it also relieves feelings of stress. A calm person is a person who is vibrating at a higher frequency.

★ Spend time in nature- Being in nature is a great way to put yourself in a more positive frame of mind, and to thus increase your vibrations. However you choose to do this, try to make an effort to go in nature at least once a day. You can go for a walk, do some gardening, meditate outside, or even just gaze up at the sky. Doing this will give you greater clarity of mind, as well as increasing your vibrational frequency.

★ Be aware of the information you are ingesting- everything you read and listen to has an effect on your energy. When we choose to watch films, TV shows, and read newspapers we can be bombarded with a tidal wave of negativity and fear that really lowers our vibrations to a very low level. Although it's important to know what's going on in the world, we need to be mindful about where we get our information from. Any form of entertainment, be it music, video games or film, that has a focus on pain, fear and anger can do the same. If you wish to raise your vibrations than you really need to be very mindful of everything you read, watch and listen to.

★ Eat fruits, vegetables, and drink water- Food and drink are essential parts of life giving energy. Eating fresh food and drinking plenty of water ensures that you are getting all the nutrients you need, as well as helping to flush out the toxins in your body; thus raising your vibration. The old saying of you are what you eat is very apt. If you choose to eat food that is full of chemicals, additives and sweeteners, then you'll be having a negative effect on your health and the energy frequency of your being. When you choose to eat healthier, fresher food you will really be looking after every aspect of your being.

★ A lovely method is to visualise your breath as different colours. As you breathe in, imagine your inhalation is coloured pink and gold. These colours are linked to the angelic realm and will help to increase the vibrations of your being. When you exhale, imagine all the negativity and toxins within your body coming out as black or grey. Take 3-5 deep breaths whilst visualising this every day, and it will definitely have a marked effect on the frequency of your energy.

Make a conscious effort to work on these things every day, and you will be making a focused effort on raising your vibration in preparation for angelic connection and communication. The next step of the process is to invite them into your life and your home.

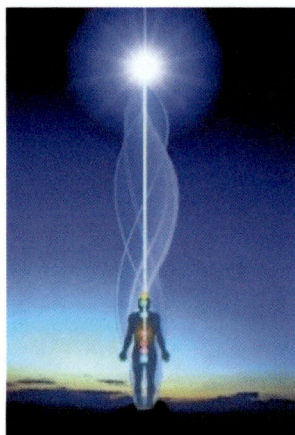

Chapter Six

Welcoming Them to You

As I mentioned previously, we all have angels with us all the time. Angels do not live up in the sky, perched on a fluffy white cloud whilst they play the harp. Angels are with you every moment of the day, whether you are aware of their presence or not. Just because you can't see them with your physical eyes, doesn't mean they don't exist. For thousands of year's people thought the Earth was flat and that sailors would fall off the edge if they sailed too close to the horizon. Scientists used to believe that the atom was the smallest particle known to man, until they split it open and found a whole heap of unexpected things inside. Our eyesight is limited, for we cannot see infrared or ultra violet rays. Our hearing is limited, for we can only hear certain pitches. And yet, there are still people who claim that if they can't see or hear something it doesn't exist. If history has taught us anything it's that we don't know everything, and that we are continually discovering things which we thought were nonsense. Angels are with you all the time, regardless of what your senses may tell you. However, there are ways in which you can consciously bring more angels to you, as well as deepening your own sense of angelic connection. These things will be examined in this chapter.

Angel Altar

An angel altar is a lovely way to establish a strong and powerful link to the angelic realms. It can be as simple or as elaborate as you like, but you don't need to worry about spending out lots of money. You can place items on there that you have found within nature for example, like feathers and shells; anything that makes you feel closer to the angels. The altar can be placed anywhere in the home, but ideally should be placed somewhere peaceful where you are able to open your mind and heart to the angels. If you are unable to have a permanent altar due to a lack of space in your home, you can also create a portable one. Place all your items in a special box and unpack them whenever you feel drawn to connecting and communicating to the angels. Creating an angel altar indicates to the angels that you are ready to connect with them, as well as engaging in communication. When creating your own angel altar, you can experiment with placement, items and the layout of it, to ensure that you feel it's a space that you can work with. Here are some suggestions of what you could include to help you get started:

- ★ A large white candle
- ★ A statue or figurine of an angel
- ★ At least two different fragrances from incense, essential oils, flowers, or scented candles
- ★ A few crystals to aid your angelic connection (more on crystals below)
- ★ Pictures of angels

Your angel altar can be the place you go to for connecting with the angels in any way, as well as a space for meditation.

Angel Vision Board

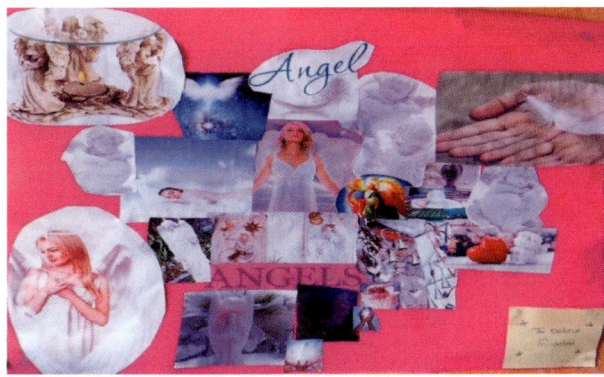

A vision board is a special arrangement of images that helps you to connect further with the angels, and can also be used to set intentions for all the good things you want to attract into your life: new home, relationship, job or more friends for example. It can be added to your altar or placed in another significant place around the home. You can make one yourself by getting a piece of A3 or A2 card, magazines, scissors and glue. Find images within the magazines that remind you of angels, as well as anything that links to things you wish to bring into your life, and cut them out. Arrange the pictures on the card with a central angel picture in the centre, like a white feather for example, and then place the others around this. When placing down the things you wish for yourself, ensure you connect inside to the emotions you would feel if you had the things you desired. Angels respond to the intentions you hold, so it's important to feel the love, happiness and gratitude that you would experience.

Crystals

Crystals are an effective tool for helping you to connect with the angelic realm. If you are new to working with crystals, do not be intimidated or worried; it's really very simple! First of all, you need to ensure that you cleanse your crystals. They are highly susceptible to energy, and if anyone has handled the crystal at any time who may have been experiencing lower energies, then these would've affected the gem. By cleansing the crystal, you are ensuring that all of these negativities are removed from its structure, so you can work with it in a safe and effective way. There are many ways to cleanse crystals, and a lot is dependent on the type of crystal you have, as some do not respond well to certain types of cleansing. The methods are:

1. Soak newly bought crystals in salty water for three days, before rinsing them thoroughly and putting them out in the sun to dry. You can use seawater for this method. Purified water with Himalayan rock salt is more effective than tap water with table salt.

2. Place them under running lukewarm water for three to five minutes. Some crystals do not like being placed in water, especially the softer ones like angelite.

3. Expose them to the smoke of an incense stick. Incense that has herbal origins is the most effective, like cedar, juniper or pine tree. White sage is also a great purifier. Place the crystal in the smoke and allow it to pass over the gem for a good five minutes.

4. Bury them in the earth. This method should not be used when there is iron present in the composition of the crystal as a dominant element, e.g., hematite and tiger iron. Especially unrefined energies can be taken out of the crystal in this way. It can be a sort of a rebirth for the particular crystal to be put back in the embrace of the earth - the environment which it has been taken from originally.

5. Placing them out during a full moon. Allowing the light of the full moon to wash over the crystals is

another effective cleansing method. The crystals can be left out overnight, even if it's cloudy.

Once the crystal has been cleansed, you need to charge it up. As with clearing, there are several methods that you can use for this, and you can use the one which you feel most comfortable with. With all methods of charging, first set your intention and state silently or aloud that you are doing this to charge your crystal for the best and highest good of all concerned. After your stone is charged, thank the Divine by whatever name you know it for assisting in charging your stone.

1. The rays of the Sun or Moon- the rays that come off both of these celestial bodies are both energising and good for clearing. Find a safe place to put your crystal for at least 24 hours, but no longer than a week. The colours of some crystals may fade in sunlight, so for them it may be more effective to bathe them in moonlight. If you're unsure, go for the latter option.
2. Stones that charge other stones- some crystals are great at energising others! Place your crystal on a cluster or a large piece of amethyst, quartz, selenite or carnelian for 24 hours, or until you feel it is at full energy.
3. Plants- place your chosen crystal amongst the leaves of a healthy plant for 24 hours or more to charge it.

There are five crystals in particular that will help you connect to the angels. These are:

★ Angelite: if you're only going to buy one crystal for angel work, this is the one to choose. Its actual name is Blue Anhydrite, but it's typically known by its metaphysical name of angelite. This is due to the fact that it carries the strongest angel vibrations of all the crystals available. Working with this stone can help you to calm any nerves you may have about working with angels, as well as creating a sense of peace for you to do so. It also helps to clear any blocks you may have inside that may hinder your angelic connection and intuition. Keeping it with you at all times can help to heal any spiritual or psychic blocks, so that you can fully open up the angels and their guidance.

★ Blue Celestite: this crystal has a strong angelic vibration. Working with it will heighten your consciousness, so that you are able to communicate with beings from higher realms.

When you wish to communicate with the angels, place it in your receptive hand, keep in on your lap, or place it upon your altar while you do so. Ask the angels any questions you wish to know, and be open to the answers that will come.

★ Larimar: this is a strong meditative stone which allows for clear connections with the higher realms. It allows you to hear and understand the words of the angelic beings more clearly. Communicating your own needs and questions will be an easier process for you too. Working with it will help you to release any earthly fears and blocks in order for you to reach a higher level of spirituality. It also increases your clairvoyant capabilities, so that you can hear your angels more.

★ Lepidolite: Meditating with this stone makes connecting with the angels less of a struggle for you, due to its ability to raise your brainwaves. Using it means the mind is more receptive, and it'll support you in reaching a higher level of consciousness. It strengthens your clairvoyance, which means angelic connection will be easier for you.

★ Danburite: this stone has very strong energy, so may be a bit intense for you to work with. It has a very high vibration, and is great for removing big blocks from your life, help you to more joy, and to open the way for more spiritual growth. Working with this crystal helps to relieve stress, worry and fear that may get in the way of you hearing you angels and working with them.

In general most angel focused crystals will be coloured blue, green, pink/lavender, or white/clear. Most angel stones are will work to accomplish three things: calm and ease fears, elevate consciousness, and open the upper chakras. Carry them, wear them, and keep them in your meditation space. Keep in mind that the smaller the stone the closer you need to keep it to your body because it will have a smaller energy field.

Angel Cards

Angel cards, also known as oracle cards, are a tool that helps you to communicate directly with the angels. In turn they can then send you the guidance, inspiration and comfort that you need to keep moving along your path. You don't need to be working as a psychic or a medium to use these cards, all you have to do is set your intention and ask for their assistance. The messages the angels give you are always very loving and supportive, so that you can make the choices and change you need to in order to be happier and more balanced in your life. Angel cards are not the same as tarot cards, the only similarity is that both cards can be laid out in spreads in order to focus on a specific issue. Using angel cards is a real collaborative process between the angels and the reader. For the reader is not only interpreting the cards that are drawn themselves, but is also channelling the messages from the angels using their clair abilities that were mentioned earlier. In this way, most of the messages are coming from the angelic realm rather than from the person doing the reading.

When choosing a deck to buy, intuition is everything. You need to have a deck that you will feel happy and comfortable working with, so going with your instincts about which deck is the right one for you will ensure you work with the most suitable one. The right deck should give you a deep feeling of peace and a spiritual connection. The images and affirmations on the cards should also speak to you in some way.

Once you have the chosen the deck you want to work with, you need to clear the cards. All oracle cards are very sensitive to energy, so they need to be cleared of any energy they may have absorbed during the process of manufacture. Hold the deck in your non-dominant hand (the one you don't write with), as this is the hand that receives energy. Make a fist with your other hand, the one which sends energy, and knock the deck of cards once. This will clear out any old energy and ensures they are now in a neutral state, ready to be energised with your own vibrations. You can also pass your hand over the deck and say *"God and the angels, please clear away any lower or negative energies that may be held within this deck. And so it is."*

Once you have done this, you can then infuse the cards with your own energy. This is done by briefly touching each card in turn whilst in a fan hold or by picking each one up individually. Fan the cards out with the artwork facing towards you. As you do so, consider any prayers or intentions which you may wish to bestow upon the cards. For example, you could say:

"I call upon God and the angels, and I ask that all of the readings which I do with these cards be accurate and insightful, as well as bringing blessings of love to everyone involved. Help me to stay connected to my higher self so that I may clearly hear, see, and feel all messages that channel through me. And so it is."

You can also ask for help with anything that you feel you may be lacking in to give readings to yourself and others; whether it be confidence, self-belief, empathy, and so on. Your cards are now cleared and consecrated, and ready for you to use.

Shuffle the deck as best as you can until you are happy. As you do so, think of a question or area of concern with which you are seeking guidance with. The angels can hear your thoughts, so you can do this inside your mind if you wish. When pulling cards from the deck, try not to over think the process too much. You are allowing your intuition and higher self to guide you in this, as the angels will draw you to the cards which are most suited to your query. You can draw just one card to give you the answers you seek, or you can pull more and arrange them into a spread. The most common of these is the three card spread:

This spread can be used to show you either the past, present, future; or can show you the problem you're experiencing, the action you need to take, and the most likely outcome. With each deck of cards comes a guidebook that will allow you to discover other spreads, as well as an interpretation of what the cards mean. This is a great reference point for beginners, but as you become more proficient you'll be able to rely more on your intuition for what the cards mean. Having angel cards in your home and working them is a clear sign that you wish to bring more angels into your life, and they will give you appropriate messages through the cards you pick.

Angel blessings and letters

Angel blessings are requests written to the angels upon small pieces of paper, which you then roll up like a scroll. You place these upon your altar or under your pillow for seven days, after which you burn it release the intentions out into the universe. An angel letter is literally a letter that you write to your angels. Within it you can pour out your heart about the current situations you are facing, as well as adding any requests you may have to make your life better. Both of these methods require a great deal of faith in the angelic realm. It's no use asking for something that will make your life happier, only to go and try to source it for yourself. For example, say you asked the angels to bring a new loving partner into your life, but you immediately started looking on dating websites. This action not only gives the angels no opportunity to manifest your desires, but it also shows that you do not have faith in the angel's ability to bring them into your life.

It's also worth noting that the angels know your life purpose, and they will always try to help you manifest things that are in line with that. They will bring you things you need for your highest and greatest good if you ask them to, rather than simply things that you need. This means you can't just ask them to help you win the lottery! If you ask the angels to help bring more abundance into your life then you may end up winning some money, but only if it's in line with your greater life purpose. It also doesn't matter what words you use in your blessing or letter, what's important is the intention behind the words. The angels will respond to pure pleas from your heart, so open it up and let the words pour out. The sit back, and notice any signs that may come your way.

There are other ways to feel as though you are bringing the angels closer to you, and a key one is discussed in the next chapter: meditation.

Chapter Seven
Meditation

Meditation is a valuable tool in connecting to the angels. By closing off your dominant senses, as well as calming your breathing and mind, you can open up to the higher realms and receive their guidance. So many people who have never meditated before really worry about engaging in this spiritual practice, and believe it's going to be impossibly difficult. The truth is that it's not hard at all, and the benefits of engaging with it are numerous. The goal of meditation is to focus and quiet your mind, eventually reaching a higher level of awareness and inner calm. Meditating will bring you:

★ Increased positivity
★ Boost of the immune system
★ Decreases pain sensitivity
★ Increases memory

★ Improves attention
★ Decreases stress
★ Decreases anxiety
★ Decreases depression

And that's before you've even connected to the angelic realm! Not only this but, it may come as a surprise to learn that you can meditate anywhere and at any time, allowing yourself to access a sense of tranquillity and peace no matter what's going on around you. You don't have to be inside a special religious or spiritual building, or sitting cross legged on a mat. I will discuss specific meditations you can do further on in the book, but for now let's just focus on the basics:

1. Prepare to meditate: It's advisable to choose a meditation area that is both calm and peaceful. You don't want to be interrupted by either people or technology of any kind; in this sense you'll be able to focus on the task at hand. The space doesn't have to be very large, just somewhere you know you won't be disturbed for the duration of the session. Turn off al TV's, phones and computers. If you have music playing in the background, ensure that it is gentle and repetitive in nature, so that it won't break your concentration. You could also perhaps consider purchasing a small indoor water fountain. The sound of trickling water proves to be extremely soothing. The room doesn't have to be completely silent however; there will be noises from outside that you won't be able to stop. However, whether it's the sound of a car, or a dog barking, these are actually

beneficial for meditation practice, for they train the mind to allow these noises to float past but not to give your attention to them. Another option is to meditate outside. So long as you're safe, and not near any busy roads or another loud noise, you may find it very relaxing to sit under a tree for example.

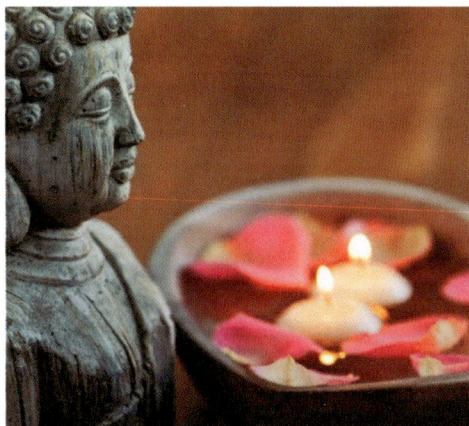

2. Wear comfortable clothes: During the meditation practice, you are aiming to calm the mind and block out any external factors of any kind. If you are wearing restrictive or uncomfortable clothing of any kind, this may hinder you from doing this. It's best to wear loose and comfortable clothes, and to also remove your shoes. If the temperature in the environment is on the cool side, make sure you are wearing a cardigan or sweater. Being cold will distract you from the task at hand.

3. Decide how long you want to meditate for: It's important to know how long you want to meditate for before you start. Those who have been doing it for a long time may recommend you meditate twice a day for twenty minutes, but beginners can do as little as five minutes once a day. You should try to meditate at the same time each time you do it: whether five minutes at lunchtime, or fifteen minutes first thing in the morning. Once you have decided the length of session, stick to it. Do not abandon it just because you feel it isn't working for you. Meditation, like anything new, takes practice to master. Keep trying and don't be disheartened if it doesn't work for you straight away. Rather than checking your watch every few seconds, consider setting yourself a gentle alarm to inform you when your time has finished.

4. Sit comfortably: You will be sitting for a period of time, so it's vital that you are as comfortable as possible. Traditionally, those who meditate will sit on a cushion in a position called the lotus, which involves the full crossing of the legs with feet on the opposite thigh or calf muscle. But this position can be difficult to get into, let alone maintain. Instead, try to find a position to sit in where your back is as straight as it possibly can be, and you are comfortable. You can either sit on the floor with a comfortable cushion underneath you, or in a chair that has a solid high back to it. You can either sit with your hands resting on your knees, palms facing upwards, or hanging down by your sides; whatever is the most comfortable for you.

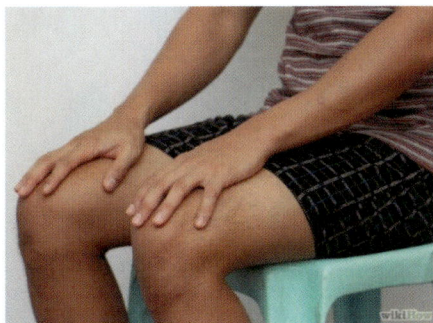

"Meditating allows you to open your conscious min to the subconscious, and the higher realms. Away from meditation you struggle to hear us because of the noise of your world. By stopping and unlocking that door inside your mind, we can connect to you easier and with greater volume. Once you start to connect to us in this was the blessings will be beyond all of your wildest dreams!"

As you move through the book you will find various meditations you can use in order to help you connect to the angels. Try them and see which one works best for you, for different people prefer different methods. Regardless of this, know that by engaging in meditation on a regular basis you will be able to create a close bond with the angelic realm, even to the point that you will eventually be able to communicate with them!

Chakras

First of all, let's start with a meditation to help you open and clear your chakras. Chakra is a Sanskrit word that means wheel or disk. They are wheels of energy that run through your body, and there are seven dominant ones that we will focus on. These run from the base of your spine right up to the crown of your head, and each one of these wheels of energy corresponds to big nerve centres within the body. The importance of this cannot be underestimated, because each of the seven main chakras contains bundles of nerves and major organs as well as our mental, emotional, and spiritual states of being. Since everything within the body is moving, it's essential that our seven main chakras stay open and aligned. If there is a blockage, energy cannot flow. Think of something as simple as a water drain. If you allow too much rubbish to go into the drain, it will back up with water, stagnate and eventually bacteria and mould will start to grow. So is too with our bodies and the chakras.

Keeping a chakra open and flowing may not be as easy keeping a drain clear, but it's easier when you have an awareness of your body, emotions and mental states. For example, let's say a woman's partner is cheating on her and she finds out. She's absolutely devastated and can't stop crying, which is so intense that she gets a hacking cough. In this instance, both her heart and throat chakras need a good clear out to help heal the cough that is affecting her so badly. She literally feels heartbroken, and she also perceives that she is unable to say the words that are going round and round her head. Although clearing her chakras won't change what's happened, it will bring a certain amount of healing to her mind and body.

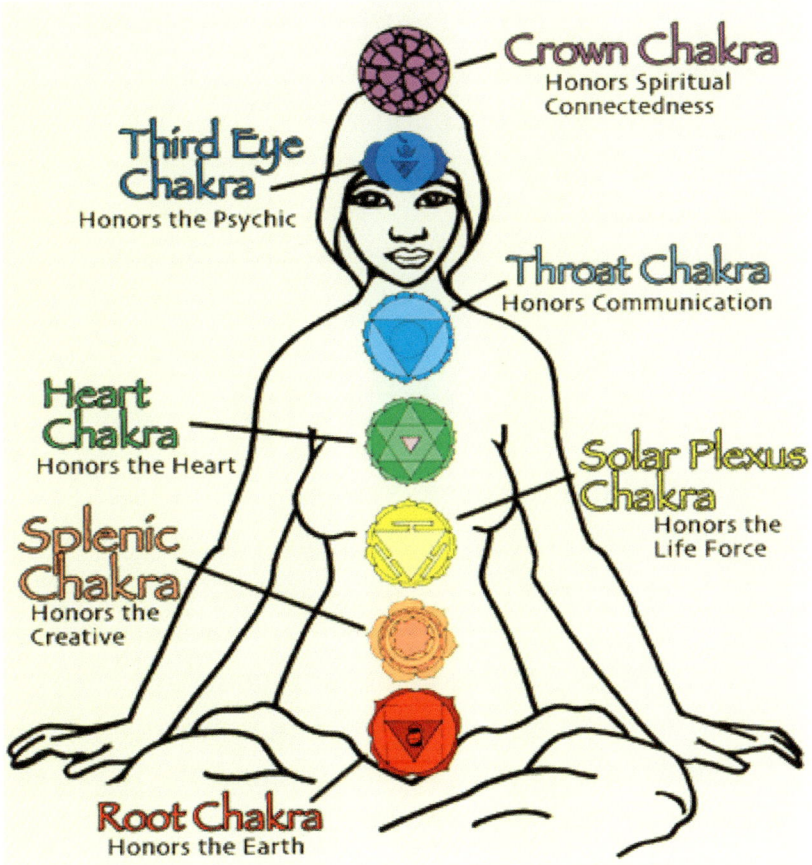

Crown Chakra
Honors Spiritual Connectedness

Third Eye Chakra
Honors the Psychic

Throat Chakra
Honors Communication

Heart Chakra
Honors the Heart

Solar Plexus Chakra
Honors the Life Force

Splenic Chakra
Honors the Creative

Root Chakra
Honors the Earth

The seven chakras relate to:

- **Root Chakra:** Found in the base of the spine, in the tailbone area. This chakra relates to the foundation of who we are and being grounded. It concerns our survival issues: financial independence, our homes and food.

- **Splenic (sacral) Chakra:** Found in the lower abdomen, about two inches below the navel. Concerns our connection with others, and the ability to accept them and all new experiences we may encounter. Centres on our sense of well-being, pleasure, sexuality and feelings of abundance.

- **Solar Plexus Chakra:** Located in the upper abdomen in the area of the stomach. It focuses on our ability to exude confidence and to feel that we are in control of our lives. It represents our sense of self-worth, self-esteem and self-confidence.

- **Heart Chakra:** This is in the centre of our chest, just above our physical heart, and is completely focused on our ability to love. It represents our sense of joy, inner peace and all aspects of love.

- **Throat Chakra:** Found in the throat, the throat chakra is our ability to communicate in whatever form we feel drawn to. It centres on our truth, communication and the self-expression of our feelings.

- **Third Eye Chakra:** Located in the forehead between the eyes, this is our ability to focus and see the bigger picture. It symbolises our intuition, wisdom, imagination, as well the ability to think and make decisions.

- **Crown Chakra:** Found right at the top of the head, this represents our ability to be fully spiritually connected. It links to our ability to see beauty inside and out, feelings of peace and bliss, and our spiritual connection.

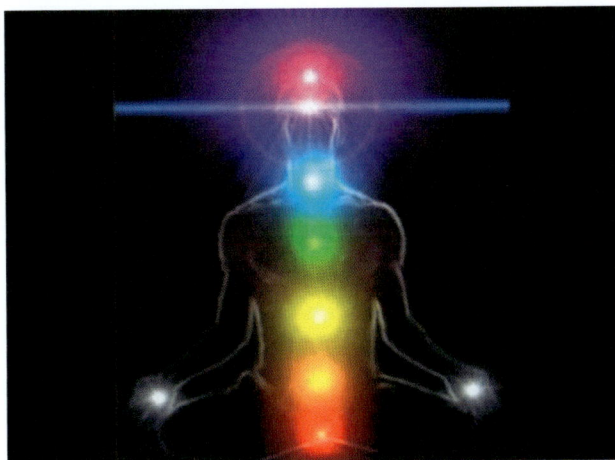

As a spiritual person, it's very tempting to focus predominately on the third eye and crown chakras, but it's important to understand that all of the chakras are connected and interlinked. If we don't focus on opening and clearing all the chakras, then none of them will be balanced fully. Consequently, our emotional, mental, physical and spiritual health will not be whole and healthy as it could be.

It's also worth noting here the importance of not only the chakras within the physical body, but the aura that surrounds it. The aura is the electromagnetic field that surrounds you and every living organism on the planet. It consists of a collection of electro - magnetic energies of varying densities that come from the physical body of a living person. These particles of energy are suspended around the healthy human body in an oval shaped field. This "auric egg" emits out from the body approximately 2-3 feet (1 metre on average) on all sides. It extends above the head and below the feet into the ground. There are several layers to the aura. Each one has its own subtle frequency, but are connected to each other. They can have a powerful effect on a person's feelings, emotions, thinking, behaviour, and health. If there is therefore an imbalance on one level, there will be a negative impact on other areas.

It is possible to see an aura, although like every spiritual activity it takes practice. The easiest way is to have someone stand against a white blank background. Look at this person but relax your gaze and let your focus soften. You might be able to see a smudgy grey outline around the person's body: the aura. With time and practice, it is possible to see colours within this energy field around the body, and each colour relates to different emotions, as well as physical symptoms. The basics are:

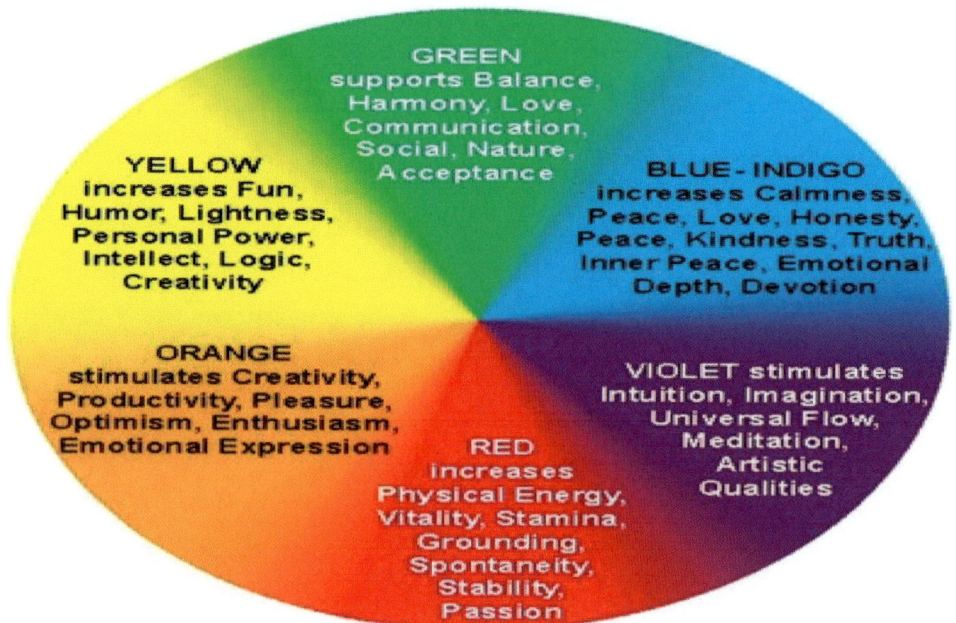

GREEN supports Balance, Harmony, Love, Communication, Social, Nature, Acceptance

YELLOW increases Fun, Humor, Lightness, Personal Power, Intellect, Logic, Creativity

BLUE-INDIGO increases Calmness, Peace, Love, Honesty, Peace, Kindness, Truth, Inner Peace, Emotional Depth, Devotion

ORANGE stimulates Creativity, Productivity, Pleasure, Optimism, Enthusiasm, Emotional Expression

RED increases Physical Energy, Vitality, Stamina, Grounding, Spontaneity, Stability, Passion

VIOLET stimulates Intuition, Imagination, Universal Flow, Meditation, Artistic Qualities

To help open and cleanse your chakras of any stagnant energy that could transmute into physical symptoms in the body (such as pain and illness), you can work with this chakra clearing meditation once a week. For effective meditation practice, record yourself reading through the guidelines below, and then play them back when you are ready to mediate. In this sense, you can fully focus on the process and not be distracted by having to continuously read the next step. This is the same for each of the meditations featured in this book. Start by working through the preparation list which is laid out above. When you comfortable and ready, you may begin:

1. Close your eyes and start by focusing on your breath. Inhale deeply through the nose and down into your stomach, before exhaling slowly. Do this five times before you move onto the next step. Breathing like this calms you down, quietens your mind, and prepares you for meditation.
2. Imagine a ball of white light underneath your feet. This ball of light glows softly and emits a beautiful feeling of peace and love. This is light from the Divine, and it is safe for you to work with.
3. Inhale and imagine this white light entering the soles of your feet and slowly travelling up your legs. You may feel a tingling sensation, some warmth or nothing at all; each reaction is perfectly normal.

Keep imagining this light travelling up your legs until it reaches the base of your spine.

4. Here it finds a ruby red flower, closed tight in a bud. As the white light reaches this flower, the petals slowly start to open one by one. Once the flower is fully in bloom, it begins to slowly spin freely. Your root chakra is now open and clear.

5. The white light then travels up again to your lower abdomen, just below your belly button. There is an orange flower located here and again it's shut in a tight bud. Yet again the flower starts to unfurl as the white light of the Divine illuminates it; opening up and slowly spinning. Your sacral chakra is now open and clear.

6. As the white light moves up to your stomach area it finds a yellow bud. Lighting up this delicate flower, the petals ease open and the whole flower circles round. Your solar plexus chakra is now open and clear.

7. At the centre of your chest is a green flower, shut tight. The bright white light moves up to this bud, shining and encouraging it open. As it does so, the centre of the flower is soft pink, and it begins to spin. Your heart chakra is now open and clear.

8. The white light of the Divine moves up your body once more, where it encounters a light blue flower at your throat, closed tight. Shining upon it, the petals open one by one and the whole flower moves round. Your throat chakra is now open and clear.

9. At the centre of your forehead, between your eyes, is a violet flower with its petals closed. The pure white

light illuminates the flower and it unfurls, spinning slowly as it does so. Your third eye chakra is now open and clear.

10. Finally, the white light reaches the top of your head, where there is an indigo flower closed tight. The white light bursts through the top of your head, and as it does so, the flower opens up and spins round. Your crown chakra is now open and clear.

11. The white of the Divine cascades down over your body like a beautiful waterfall, raining down drops of love all over your body. As it reaches the floor, the light connects to the ball of light that is still at your feet. The white light moves through your body again: up your legs, through each one of the seven chakras, and out the top of your head. This time the light does not fall back down, but is sent upwards to Heaven, returning back to the Creator from which it came.

12. Finally, one by one, each one of your beautiful flowers softly closes back down. This starts at the top of your head with your crown chakra; down to your third eye; your throat; your heart; solar plexus; sacral; and finally the root chakra. All flowers are now closed, as are your chakras. They are all now clear, and your whole system is balanced and healthy.

13. Gently wriggle your fingers and toes to bring your mind back to the full consciousness. When you feel ready, open your eyes. Drink a glass of water to help flush out any toxins that may have been released into your system from the meditation.

Feedback:

* ★ Did you have any apprehension or worries before you started the meditation? If so, what were they?

* ★ What did you feel during the process? Did you have any physical or emotional sensations?

★ Did the meditation go as you thought it would or was it different? In what way?

★ How did you feel afterwards?

Making the commitment to yourself to regularly clear out your chakras is a very beneficial gift to give yourself. Not only does it prepare you for meditating so you can get used to the process, but it also means that your whole body is ready to connect to the higher angelic realms; physically, mentally, emotionally and spiritually. As we progress along the process of connecting with the angels, you will encounter further meditations that will develop your abilities.

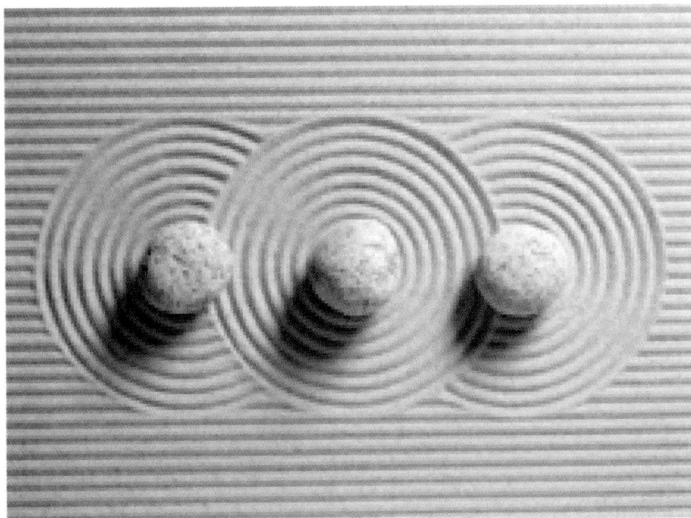

Chapter Eight

Healing with the Angels

One of the miraculous gifts the angels can bestow upon us is their ability to help us heal. Whether it's physical, emotional, mental or spiritual healing you require, it does not alter the fact that once you ask the angelic realm for help, it will be given to you. The angels are with the people of this planet to help us live in total peace and happiness, and they understand that being unhealthy in any sense really takes this away from you. By helping to restore you back to full health, they are helping you to be whole inside and out.

Physical Healing

In Chapter Four I introduced you to the Archangels, and Raphael is the one to call on when you require healing for the physical body. You can ask him to heal yourself when you are ill or in pain, or you can ask him to send healing to someone else who is in need of it. If the healing is for yourself, you can ask him within your mind, aloud, or write it down; choose which method you feel is most appropriate for you at the time. Once you have called on his help, be open to the images or thoughts that may suddenly come into your mind like a spiritual download. He may send you suggestions on how you can improve your health, the remedies you could take, or he may come to your during sleep whilst you are dreaming. You may intuitively hear him telling you to get medical assistance, if you haven't already done so. Raphael works closely with all those in the medical profession, even if they are not aware of his presence, so do not worry about any conflict of interest.

"I am the angel of healing and, by working with me, I can help you to channel my great power to those in need of it; including yourself. My supply is endless, and there are no limits to who I can bring relief to. Do not fret that you may be taking my attention away from those who you deem to be more in need than yourself. If you are in pain or are suffering with an illness, it is both my duty and my pleasure to bring you the healing you need."

If you are calling on Raphael to help give healing to someone else, he will help them but he can't interfere with their free will. Even if the other person does not wish to be healed for whatever reason though, be assured that Raphael will bring them comfort and do whatever he can to help make them feel better. Always keep your faith that everything is working out according to God's divine plan, and try to keep as calm and loving as you can; this will help improve the situation for everyone involved. God knows the best methods and roads for you to head down in relation to your life plan and for each ailment. There is always divine order behind every situation that occurs, even if our minds are not able comprehend it.

If you are looking to purchase remedies for yourself or someone else, whether aromatherapy oils, crystals or flower essences, then Raphael can help you to choose the most suitable one for your needs. If you have asked Archangel Raphael for help and you are worried that he may not have heard of you (though I assure you he has), then you can look out for any unusual activity in birds. For example, you may find that a bird is staring at you or tapping at the window. You may also find a feather in a place that you wouldn't expect.

There are a number of ways in which you can ask for help with matters of health. You can;

- Say your prayer or request aloud
- Direct it straight to God, to Raphael, or to them both
- Include any religious deity that you may feel an affinity to: Jesus, Mother Mary, etc.
- Think the request in your mind
- Write it down

- Whisper the words or shout them loud
- Say the request with humbleness and reverence, or with frustration and desperation
- Demand assistance ("Please help me!"), or say it in the affirmative voice ("Thank you for your guidance and help")

What matters the most is that you ask for the help you need, not how you do it. The angels know the intentions behind the words, so speak from the heart and give voice to your deepest feelings. Visualise green light surrounding you from the tip of your toes to the top of your head. Green is the colour of healing, and placing yourself in a green bubble will prove to be very soothing and healing for you. Know that Raphael's assistance is tailor made just for you and your own needs. Whether he gives immediate assistance himself or guides you to the right practitioners who'll be able to help you; know that he will always answer every request that comes to him.

If you would rather have a prayer to work with in asking Raphael for help, you can try the following:

"Archangel Raphael, I call upon you know. Please shine you healing light down upon me to rid my body of all illness, disease and pain. Take away all my sadness and fears, and wrap your loving wings around me to make me whole once more. And so it is."

You can also meditate with Raphael to help give you the physical healing that you are in need of. Sit in a space that is quiet and where you won't be disturbed. Light a white or green candle. Prepare to meditate and close your eyes. Relax your mind by focusing on your breathing, and picture Raphael coming to you. Open your mind to the messages which he gives you. Your mind may try to tell you that you're just making it up and it's not real, but try to be as non-judgemental as you can. Ask him any questions you may have and not dismiss the answers that will come to mind. Once you have finished asking the questions you need answering and receiving the messages from Raphael, imagine a bright green light beaming down on you and filling every cell of your body. This light will give you the healing you need. Thank Raphael for helping you, and once you have ended the meditation, write down any messages which you received.

Be aware that when you ask Raphael to help heal you, there are times when you may not receive the healing you expect. In her book You Can Heal Your Life (Hay House, 2004), writer Louise Hay explores the relationship between the mind and the body. She explores the way that limiting thoughts and ideas control and constrict us, and offers a powerful key to understanding the roots of physical diseases and discomforts. Sometimes you may find that you ask Raphael to help you heal physically, but he will bring emotional issues and concerns to the surface instead. This is because it is the emotional issue that is the real root behind the physical problem, and you need to concentrate on healing this first. Note that this isn't always the case, and Raphael will bring physical healing to all who call on him. Just be aware that his methods may not follow the route you expect! Like all angels though, Raphael knows God's plan for you and will always do what is the best for your highest and greatest good.

Emotional Healing

Emotional health is just as important as physical. For those who experience any kind of emotional issue but push it down rather than deal with it, they will tend to find themselves dealing with ill health in a relatively short space of time. When you do not heal and clear the emotional traumas which you have been through, you will find that they will manifest as physical disease and pain. The negativity in your body needs to come out somehow; like bubbles in liquid, they will rise to the surface.

Archangel Chamuel and his team of the angels of love can help you to heal emotionally by bringing you the energies of unconditional love, beauty and compassion. Within any situation that requires heartfelt communication in order to heal, these angels will be available to help you. Once you have called on them for help and given them your specific request, they will be able to heal your heart and make your life harmonious in every way. Archangel Chamuel can help to ease tension and nervousness, and can be called upon to ease and manage worry and anxiety and bring about inner-peace. Archangel Chamuel is known as the protector of the weak and defender of the down-trodden, and may be called upon for comfort, protection and intervention.

Ultimately, emotional healing starts by developing your heart chakra, although many are afraid to do so. Past pains and betrayals can clamp a person's heart shut and they are so terrified of getting hurt again that they never give their love to anyone; not even themselves. But if you are able to heal this trauma and put it behind you, you will find that you will end up with immense feelings of peace and happiness within. Working with Chamuel can help bring healing to all of the relationships in your life, so that each one have open channels of communication, trust and love for all involved. He can also help move through life changing situations easier, including conflicts, divorce, bereavement and job loss.

To call upon Archangel Chamuel for the support and guidance you need in helping to heal your emotions, you can say the following;

"Dearest Divine Archangel Chamuel,

I love you, I honour you and I appreciate you. I ask for your assistance today. Help me to stay open in a state of love through all that I experience and I ask to see the love and godliness in all whom I encounter.

I am eternally grateful for all that you do for me. Thank you, and so it is."

You can also meditate to call upon Chamuel and ask him to give you them emotional healing you are in need of. Light a pink candle and hold some rose quartz in your hand. Sit comfortably and relax. When you feel ready, call upon Archangel Chamuel. Say *"Blessed Archangel Chamuel, please help me with (your situation). Heal my heart chakra and let love flow in my life. Thank you for your help with this and all that you do. And so it is."* Take some deep breaths and continue to relax. Let your thoughts flow freely without censorship or judgement. Let go of any unwanted memories by imagining them as black energy leaving your body when you exhale. Pay attention to the thoughts that will come from Chamuel to help you heal.

"Your heart is so big and yet so fragile. You seek to give your precious love out to others and, although this is an extremely blessed act, you will always risk your heart coming back bruised in the process. It is easy to shut yourself off from love when this happens; build up the walls around your heart so you can no longer be hurt, but this seeks to only really hurt yourself. Allow me to gently

tear down the walls and let love pour back into you. Let me show you that there is compassion, decency and love within the world, and it is all there to bring peace into your soul."

Spiritual Healing

Have you ever felt you are so much more than your outer activity and current life seems to indicate? Have you ever had the sense that inside of you somewhere is this great being of Light and power? That you had a deeper purpose? If so, then you already have an awareness of the wonderful being of Light that you truly are - your Higher Self! By reconnecting with your Higher Self, you will experience more joy, happiness, peace and abundance. The flip side of this is being rooted in the ego. The ego is an illusion based entity created within the human mind. The ego is your human conscious that allows you to function within the world, but it's not you. Your ego is the negative voice inside that is based upon fear- one that bases itself on separateness, judgements, greed and anxiety; but it's not you. How do I know that your ego self, your mind, isn't you? Consider the fact that your mind never ever stops talking, a chattering monkey that has an opinion on everyone and everything. You are not your ego because you are the witness, the observer of the thoughts. Once you fully realise this astonishing fact about yourself, you will see that you are indeed a spiritual being having a human experience. That your body is but a shell that encases the divine light of your being. You are not your ego, you are your Higher Self.

The angels understand fully that we all have free will, and they will never challenge our right to make our own choices in life, but they may challenge patterns of behaviour and belief system that are no longer serving you. Living within the ego means that ultimately we may end up becoming stuck in dysfunctional emotional baggage that stops us from living our life to our own highest and greatest good. Archangel Zadkiel is the angel who can help unchain us from our own fear based baggage so that we can truly spread our wings and fly. Zadkiel is the guardian of something called the 'Violet Flame', which you can use to help transform your energy from fear based ego thoughts to the love of the Higher Self. St. Germain gave us this flame, to use for purification and cleansing of our energy fields, our auras, and our bodies. It is the highest frequency light, and can raise our vibration by clearing any negative energy we are holding. Since Archangel Zadkiel is in charge of the Violet Flame, all you need to do is call on him to help you clear. You can say: *"I now invoke*

Archangel Zadkiel and the Violet Flame to cleanse and heal me on all levels of my four body system-mental, spiritual, emotional and physical." Then imagine seeing this violet flame coming up through your feet from the earth, and breathe it into your heart, fanning it out to every level of your body and into your energy field. Sit quietly for a few moments breathing in the Violet Flame, intending to release anything that no longer serves you. When you feel complete, thank Archangel Zadkiel and the Violet Flame for their loving assistance. Do this whenever you are having trouble with negative feelings you want to release, like anger, resentment, hurt, or depression.

"You have had many lifetimes upon the Earth, dear one. Each incarnation has taught you many lessons and helped you to grow and develop. However, not every lifetime has been joyful or filled with love. There has been pain, betrayals and more turmoil then you could ever bear. It is easy to get stuck down in the heaviness of human life, to believe that your human body is weighed down by the mire of human suffering. And yet, within each and every one of you, is a pure being of light. You are not your body. Know that each experience, whether good or bad, is a lesson to be learnt. But it is not there to pull you down and make you forget who you really are. Let me help to open your eyes to your own miraculous and beautiful light. Doing so will open your heart, and allow your spiritual being to expand with love and light to all."

Distant Healing

The world can be a scary and truly depressing place at times. You turn on the television or pick up a newspaper and you are hit by a tidal wave of tragedy, pain and desperation. At times like this it easy to feel powerless and overwhelmed with it all, but there is something you can do. Working with Archangel Sandalphon, who is known as the angel of the Earth, you can send distant healing to both individuals and situations around the world. You can request that remote, transformational, angelic healing be sent to the needy, the grieving and the bereaved, the desperate, and to all those who are suffering or afraid. When you see a disaster unfolding, or come across the aftermath, you can summon Sandalphon to help send the healing needed to all those involved in it. It doesn't matter if the disaster is natural or manmade, based on war or the effects of famine, the healing will be sent just the same. You can also call upon Sandalphon to help bring healing to friends, family, and anyone else we know who may be in need of angelic assistance.

The easiest way to send healing remotely is by prayer. An example of this would be, *"Blessed Archangel Sandlaphon, angel of remote healing, I ask that you assist me in sending healing, love and comfort to (insert the name of someone, or a place affected by tragedy). Help them to feel the grace and love of the Divine within their hearts so that they may know peace. Bring them the healing they need in order for them to feel healthy and whole once more. Wrap your loving wings around them and hold them close in angelic love. I am eternally grateful for your love and help. And so it is."*

You can also send distant healing to those in need by forming an angelic energy sphere. Focus all of your intentions and imagination on the place or people you want the healing to be sent to. See them in your mind's eye and say their name within your head. Once you have done this, you then need to summon the angels, which you do simply by saying the word "angels" in your mind. Visualise a sphere of energy forming between your hands, which are slightly apart in front of you. You can imagine this orb of energy in whichever colour you feel is most suitable: green for healing; pink for love; or even rainbow coloured, as Sandalphon works with red, orange, yellow, green, blue, indigo and violet. Once you can clearly visualise this energy sphere between your hands, raise your arms above your head, and open your hands, letting the sphere go. Ask that Sandalphon send this energy sphere to the person or area of the world which you want to send the healing to, and know that the archangel will take the energy where it is needed.

As mentioned previously, each one of us is born with free will, so it typically a good idea to get permission to do healing on someone before you do it. However, if this is not possible because you do not know the people involved personally, or the person is not conscious to agree (they are in a coma for example), then direct the energy to be used for the highest and greatest good of everyone involved and that it harms none. If the healing is not wanted by the recipient it simply won't be accepted by the Higher Self of said individual.

"The Earth is going through a period of transition right now, and not all the changes can appear as positive and uplifting. Watching events play out that are truly devastating and tragic can be so upsetting for you, especially when you feel powerless to help those going through them. But you are never powerless; you have the power of God within every cell of your being. Call upon me to help you remember this, and to use this power to send healing to all those involved. By shining love and light upon the world, you really are doing a most blessed miracle for all."

Relationships

Relationships of all kinds dominate all of our lives. No matter what form they take: romantic, friendship, family, work colleagues and so on; they are the place of our greatest learning and growth as human beings. Whilst you can read as many spiritual books as you like and take all the classes in the world, it is only through the daily interactions with others that you will actually be able to put into practice the beliefs and ideals that you hold dear in your heart. Relationships are a place of joy, comfort and stability when they are going well, but every partnership experiences difficulties. This is to be expected no matter who is involved, for you have at least two individuals with their own personalities, experiences and ideals. Even with your own immediate family you may find problems arise. Some people expect that this is unlikely to happen because of the blood ties between you all, but you are all still individuals and you won't get along all the time.

When conflict arises within any relationship it can cause us much unhappiness and distress on all levels. Initially you will be aware of anguish on a mental and emotional level, but they can also affect you physically and spiritually too. Dealing with any situation where there is emotional unbalance and stress will have a negative impact on your health, even if you are not aware of it. You spiritual self will also be affected as its main focus is love and harmony. Thus, experiencing troublesome relationships will leave its negative fingerprints all over your spiritual self too. Archangel Uriel is the one to call on to help heal any relationship issues you may be experiencing, as he is the angel for emotional harmony and mental clarity. If you are dealing with any kind of inner conflict, having trouble sleeping, feeling angry or dealing with volatile personal relationships, Uriel can help smooth things over. Working with ensures that you are able to keep calm, cool and collected when things around you are going crazy. He helps you to remember the true oneness of all life, and to release painful memories by applying the miracle of forgiveness.

To connect with Uriel to heal any relationship problems you may be dealing with, you can try the following meditation;

Choose a place where you will be able to meditate in peace and quiet for at least half an hour without being disturbed. Ensure that you are warm enough, but not too hot so that you won't become distracted by an uncomfortable temperature for you. Sit on a chair or on the floor so that you are comfortable and secure. Start to focus on your breath as you close your eyes. With each exhalation, visualise all the stresses and anxieties of the day being released out into the universe, and feel your body relaxing. Mentally scan your body to see if there are any areas of tension and consciously relax them by letting the stresses melt away.

See yourself now standing in a garden full of beautiful flowers. The sun is setting behind you and you can smell the heady aroma of the blooms in the dusk. You feel the warmth of the sun caressing your skin, and feel truly happy and relaxed. As the sun sinks, you are aware of a sense of anticipation in the air, although you do not feel worried or scared by this. In the darkness you are suddenly aware of an angel standing in front you. He is truly glorious and you feel in awe of his breath-taking appearance. The reason you are able to see him in the dark is that you see a flame burning in the centre of his chest. You realise that this flame is not hurting the angel in anyway, and you know that this is the symbol for Archangel Uriel. This flame is the fire of love. As you stand there, you watch the flame flickering away, and a great sense of pure love wraps itself around you. This love is like nothing you have ever felt before and you it really is the most beautiful feeling. You are totally engulfed in a blanket of love and compassion, and you feel the greatest sense of peace unlike nothing you have ever felt before.

Uriel is smiling at you and you know that you can ask him to help you with whatever is troubling you. Anything you ask of him will be acted upon, and you will be listened to without judgement. You know that you can tell him anything that is on your mind, and Uriel will help you to release your pain and worry so that you can heal. There is no rush with this process, you can take however long you need. Uriel is extremely patient and will give you all the time and space you need to resolve the problems that are upsetting you.

Once you have finished speaking to Uriel, thank him for his help and love. Having said goodbye to him, you will see both him and the garden grower fainter and less distinct around you. When you feel ready, become more aware of the room that you are sitting in. Wriggle you finger and toes to help bring your conscious mind back to your body. Count slowly down from five to one, then open your eyes. Write down any messages that Uriel gave you to help you act upon them and bring the relationship the healing it needs.

"Each relationship is a lesson for you. Either they are with you to help you grow, or you are to help them. No matter how good or bad, they are never a waste of your precious time. But, when you are ghoing through difficult times, it can be hard to understand this undeiable fact. I can help bring healing to the relationships that may be giving you turmoil and upset, if you ask me to. The relationship is with you to teach you the lessons you need to learn, and I can not take this waay until the time is right for you to move on from it, but I can make the relationship easier for

everyone involved so it does not cause unnecsaary stress to you.”

As with any issue that is causing you stress and anxiety, the angels can help you to make the situation better if you ask them to. No problem is too big or small for the angels to assist you with, so that you can have true happiness in your heart. The next chapter will show you some more ways that you can bring angelic help into your life.

Chapter Nine

How Angels Can Assist You

There are so many ways the angels can help us in our daily lives! There is no request or situation that is too big or too small for them to handle. Indeed, if there is stress, worry or unhappiness in your life, know that asking the angels to help you with the cause of this negativity will help to heal and resolve it for the greatest good of all involved. For angels are here to help bring peace and happiness to all humanity and will help to eliminate stress in whatever form it may come in for you. Let's look at some of the other ways in which you can receive angelic help and guidance.

Protection

In every walk of life you will encounter people and situations that may prove to be aggressive and harsh to you. Whether it be dealing with aggression, selfishness, hostility, or other negative traits, it can prove to be a very upsetting environment to find yourself in. When you start to connect with the angels on a regular basis you will find that a shift takes place within you, and those activities and people that you were once interested in no longer sit comfortably with you. Things such as violent or scary films, the constant bombardment of negative news and being around certain people may all now feel quite jarring to you. Instead you may find that you actively seek out more peaceful and positive people and activities which fit better with your spiritual awakening. This is quite normal, and you should always remember that those who truly matter to you won't mind what you do so long as you're happy. Those who mind what you do really don't matter.

The other thing you may have to be careful of is a thing known as psychic vampires. We are all familiar with the blood sucking versions of vampires that adorn our culture through the mediums of books, television and film, but these vampires are a different type altogether. Rather than drain your blood they drain the energy out of you and leave you feeling lethargic, tired and flat. These vampires may consciously look to take energy off people, but most are very unaware that they are doing it. In a nutshell, psychic vampires are on the hunt for energy which they get through our attention. In an ideal world, we grow from childhood to adulthood, where we go from other taking care of us to taking care of ourselves. Along the way, if that healthy maturation process doesn't quite happen we can be left as adults who are still looking for the outside world to meet our needs on any or every level. That sends people on a hunt for energy and they become absolute masters or mistresses at getting it through a variety of means. Charm, anger, desperation, presenting as a victim and pleas for help are all approaches that they can use.

The angels can help to protect you from harsh environments and people if you ask them to, so that you don't take on this negative energy yourself. The first is shielding and can be done anytime or anywhere that you need it, and it's incredibly easy to do. Before you go into a situation that may have lower energies within it ask

Archangel Michael to place a bubble of protection all around you to keep you safe. Visualise this bubble starting at your feet and going all the around you, right to the top of your head. You can also imagine this bubble of light being different colours according to the purpose you need it for:

- White light- suitable for protection against physical attack or crime of any kind. Asking for a bubble of white light will bring more angels by your side
- Pink light- only love can permeate a pink light, so this will protect you from negativity of any sort. If you find yourself in the company of people who complain, gossip, or are generally very pessimistic, then a pink bubble of light will definitely help to protect you
- Green light- used as a light for physical healing, it's suitable for anyone who is ill or injured
- Purple light- offers psychic protection. Will shield you from lower entities and psychic vampires
- Mirrored ball- When you are about to enter an environment that you know will be full of negative energy in some form, visualising a bubble that is mirrored will ensure that all of this energy is reflected away from you. This is especially good if you are feeling particularly vulnerable, if you've been unwell or have just cleared and opened your chakras for example.
- Lead shield- By visualising yourself surrounded by a lightweight lead bubble you are ensuring that you have the highest level of protection available to you.

This is particularly helpful if you are facing a situation of conflict or severe aggression, and you are feeling vulnerable or spiritually open

- Triple shield- you can visualise more than one bubble around yourself in the different colours you need so that you have all the protection that you need.

Cutting Your Cords

Whenever we experience any kind of relationship that has a basis in fear, we subconsciously create an attachment to them that is based in the fear that this person may leave us or change in some way. This then creates a spiritual leash to said person, tying us to them even if we no longer speak or see this person anymore. If you could see these leashes you would be looking at something that is similar to surgical tubing. They are hollow and energy is able to move back and forth the tube from one person to another. These cords are always based around fear, and are unhealthy for both individuals connected to them. They are not linked to love in any way or the healthy parts of a relationship, so cutting these cords doesn't mean you have to leave someone if you don't want to; it's simply cutting away the negativity that may be within a relationship. Say for example your partner is going through a really bad time and is feeling really down. Without realising it they will start to drain energy off you, and you too will end up feeling drained and tired without really knowing why. These kind of feelings cannot be perked up be caffeine or sleep either.

If you work in a profession that helps people, such as a teacher, healer or counsellor, you will find that you have a lot of cords attached to you. Therefore you should seek to cut cords after each session, or if you find yourself feeling tired without any logical explanation. And just because you've cut cords once doesn't mean they won't come back if the relationship continues to be centred on feelings of fear. Symptoms of having cords that need to be removed are:

- Unable to move on

- Unable to stop thinking or obsessing about a person

- Frequent conversations in your mind with a person

- Frequently remembering what they said in the past, feeling their ongoing judgment or criticism

- Arguments, sometimes daily in your mind with someone (these can be actual psychic arguments)

- Constant memories or emotions that arise - i.e. we used to watch that show together

- Temptation to go back to a relationship that does not serve you

- Stalking another online through social networking, watching them compulsively

- Unable to sleep, or endless processing of the past

- Deep feelings of sadness, anger, and depression around the past

- Feelings of wanting to get revenge, or constantly aware of unfair treatment

- Crying a whole lot, an emotional wreck

- Turning down other offers and invitations, stuck in the past, feeling uninterested

Archangel Michael carries with him a sword of light which is used to cut through fear and negativity. To have him cut your cords, find a quiet place where you will be alone for a few minutes. Take some deep breaths through your nose and out through your mouth. Call upon Archangel Michael to help you by saying his name aloud or in your mind. Then say,

"Archangel Michael, I call upon you now to help me heal by cutting all etheric cords that have attached themselves to me and sending them back to whom they belong to. Fill the openings with beautiful white light, and send your

loving energy to everyone involved. Thank you for your help with this, and so it is."

You may feel the cords being cut or even pulled away from your body, and you should feel a lot lighter and more peaceful once the work is completed. You may even see a picture of the person involved within your mind. You can repeat this exercise as much as you need to so that your whole self is kept at a high vibration.

Romance

The Romance Angels are a group of loving angels who help with your love life. Everyone has their own group of Romance Angels, so you don't have to worry that the Romance Angels will not be able to help you. Their sole mission in life is to help you experience love in all areas of your life, especially with romantic partners. All you have to do is invoke their assistance and they will come to help you, always.

Steps to Invoke Your Romance Angels:

1.   Say aloud or in your mind "Romance Angels please come to me now…help me feel your loving presence."

2.   Close your eyes and take a deep breath, and hold it…

3.   As you release your breath, allow yourself to feel your Romance Angels next to you, over one or both of your shoulders.

4. Ask for guidance and healing as explained below:

Once you have invoked their presence, which really means that you have accepted their help, you can ask them to stay with you always and to give you guidance, anywhere and at any time that would be helpful to you.

You can have mental conversations with your Romance Angels about your love life, and ask them what steps you can take in your life that would help increase the love and romance in your life so that you may have peace of mind and joy in your heart. Alternatively, you can write down your current romantic situation and ask your Romance Angels for signs, guidance and healing.

Another way to bring love into your life is to visualize your perfect partner coming to you with open and loving arms. His/her love is just for you and you alone. They have done the healing work that was needed for their heart to be emotionally ready to love YOU right now. See how your partner has a kind heart just like yours do and is so happy to share their life with you. Then imagine what your ideal partner's energy feels like so you will recognize them when you meet them. Close your eyes and imagine the fragrance of their skin, their gentle touch, the rhythm of their heart. Allow all your senses to recognize your perfect partner.

Tell your angels that your arms and heart are open and ready to receive your partner's love now. Say, *"I am ready to receive love and be loved."* Let them know you are ready for a relationship anchored by love, kindness and mutual respect. Say aloud, *"I am ready, willing and open to receive this beautiful love in my life NOW."*

Write this phrase down in a journal or say it to yourself a couple of times each week: *"My wonderful loving partner comes to me easily and effortlessly. They have the same kind heart, morals and goals as I do. Our love together stays strong, true and loyal. Our love is one of great friendship that grows and blossoms and fills our hearts more than we knew was possible. Together, my soulmate and I create the joyous life we deserve, one that overflows with love and gratitude more and more each day."*

Remember, the Romance Angels love you and want you to be happy. When you are happy in love, you are happy in life and everything in your life seems to flow easier and better. They may guide you to take steps in other areas of your life to increase your self-love and self-respect, which ultimately impact your love life. Receive the Romance Angels gentile messages and trust that they are here to help you.

Financially

Another big dream that a lot of people have is to be financially secure, so it's normal to wonder if the angels can help bring money into your life. The short answer to this question is yes they can, although it's unlikely to be handed to you on a plate every time and it may not take the form which you may expect. Angels are here to help us in whatever they can, but so long as it is line with our highest and greatest good. Angels operate on a vibration of love so if you ask for money to spread love in the world or come from a genuine need, they will help. If you are asking out of greed or 'just because you'd like more money', you're unlikely to receive what you ask for. The key to receiving money or any form of abundance from the angels is three simple words:

ASK ➡ **BELIEVE** ➡ **RECEIVE**

★ Ask- ask for the help you need, but believe that you are truly worthy of receiving it. Be crystal clear as to what you want, in as much detail as possible. You can say it aloud, think it within your mind, or write it down

★ Believe- feel the emotions that you'll have when the thing you have asked for comes to you: relief, joy and peace of mind. Believe in the angels too. It's no good asking for help, then going to source it yourself! Straight away you are saying to the angels that you don't actually need their help and you can sort it out yourself

★ Receive- Be open to receive what comes your way, and know it will come to you when the time is right. It may not come in the form you expect, but you will get what you need. For example, you may ask for money to buy a new car, but the angels will send you a mechanic to fix the one you have instead. If the outcome is not in line with your highest good, then you also may not receive what you expect. For example, you may want £50,000 so you can quit your job and start up your own business. Although your business may be spreading love in the world, it may not be what you signed up as a soul to do. You may need to stay in your job for stability to explore what your true purpose in life is. The Angels are on your side and are helping, but you may not get the £50,000 you asked for. Instead you will receive other gifts if you're willing – such as brilliant ideas or other opportunities.

Tips to bear in mind when asking the angels to help you with financial matters:

• Ask and then watch and wait – **notice new ideas, feelings or visions giving you directions**.

- **Abundance comes in many forms** – such as extra time, support and ideas.
- Look out for **signs** that your Angels are helping you. For example, angels leaving coins for you as reassurance when in doubt. They can be pretty inventive with signs.
- Be **thankful for the abundance** you already have in your life.
- Be thankful for any help or signs you receive.
- **Stop worrying about money** – worry only attracts more money problems.
- **Visualise abundance** and what it brings you.
- **Affirm prosperity**: *"I am a money magnet and prosperity of all kinds is drawn to me"*

The most important thing is to come from a place of love, not greed. You do deserve to be happy and comfortable, remember though that abundance doesn't always come as money; you may be rich in friendship, love, joy and laughter instead. Be open to receive. You are loved.

Moving house

It is said that moving house is one of the most stressful things you can do in your life. Certainly going through the process can prove to be extremely challenging for many different reasons: trying to find the right house, sorting our finances, and dealing with other buyers and estate agents! But, as with everything else in life, the angels can give you the help you need if you ask them to. Indeed, the angels can guide you in so many ways when it comes to moving house: finding the perfect new home; help you sell or rent your previous home; assist with financing a new residence; ease the relocation process; keep moving-related stress to a minimum; and protect your belongings during the move.

To ask for help from the angels regarding a smooth and stress-free move to a new house, you can simply ask them to help you, but there are other things you can do if you wish to make more of a focused request:

- Find a picture of a house that you would love to move into. It doesn't have to be the exact property if you're unsure, but look for one that has the features that you would love to live with: large garden, situated by a river, Victorian style, etc.
- You could also write a list of all the features and location of the house that you are dreaming of. Go into as much detail as you feel inclined to list, though bear in mind the house may be more readily available for you if you don't list the dimensions of each room and the colour scheme!
- Place the picture and/or the list by a white candle and a picture of an angel.
- Every day for as long as you feel necessary, but at least for a week, light the candle and visualise yourself living in this property, along with all the positive emotions you would have once this manifests into reality. Spend at least five minutes doing this, so that you have a clear picture in your mind and have really connected to the energy of the angelic request.
- Say these words *"Beloved angels, please help me to find and secure this property so that I can easily move in. Help the whole process go quickly and smoothly, and ensure that I obtain the property for the best possible price. Thank for your help with this and all that you do. And so it is!"*
- Blow out the candle and have faith that the angels are working on your behalf to make your request a

reality for you. Pay attention to any signs or guidance that may come your way.

Moving angels

Getting fit

How many of us have issues with losing weight and getting fit? Every January gym and fitness class memberships soar as people promise themselves that they'll shed the pounds this year, but a lot quickly tail off as the year progresses. Or you will see some people lose weight on various different diets, only to keep putting the weight back on in a matter of months after coming of said diet plans. For many people it's a constant battleground, but you must be wondering why would angels want to help you with such things as getting fit and weight loss?

Many a time, weight gain is an emotional and mental issue. We use weight as a protective barrier against our own feelings such as anger and being unable to forgive which we do not know how to handle. Sometimes our barrier increases around certain people or in certain situations too. For example, a woman may be betrayed by her partner and may subconsciously gain weight so that she deems herself unattractive. In her mind she won't now be able to get a partner and will therefore save herself from any more heartache. The weight gain is her way of feeling safe and protected. In these instances, it is the underlying emotional issues that need to be dealt with first, as trying to lose weight and get fit may prove to be unsuccessful. Unless the underlying problems are examined, a person may continue to try and self-sabotage without realising it.

Any stress or pent up feelings that are not dealt with can result in weight gain, for the body will convert these feelings into fat. If a person is able to release these feelings, the weight will also dissolve. In simpler cases, weight management is a matter of the proportion of exercise   and   diet.

Angels will help you with weight loss because they know it will bring you a greater sense of peace, and they are here to make life as peaceful as possible for you. Angels will help you get to the root cause of your weight issue so that you can honestly and lovingly release any negativity you may be holding onto. They will also send you messages repeatedly through various types of media until you take action, so there is no need to worry about missing their guidance. The angels are gentle and loving yet persistent weight   management   coaches.

Here are some ways in which you can connect with the angels or ask for their help. Do not tell them how to solve the problem as the angels know the divine life plan God has for you, and so know best how to give you the help you   need.

"Angels, I call upon you now. I ask you now to help me to get to the underlying root of my weight issue and help me heal it from the inside out. Give me the courage I need to face this honestly and lovingly, and please guide me all the way. Thank you for your help with this. And so it is."

"Angels, I call upon you now. Please help me to make healthy food and drink choices today that are the best for my health, energy, and nutritional needs. Please remove any unhealthy cravings I may have and replace them with cravings for healthy fruits and vegetables. Thank you for your help with this. And so it is."

"Dear angels, please help me choose a type of exercise that is fun for me and helps me attain my ideal weight. Keep me motivated so that I remain focused on this goal. Also, protect me from any injury I may get as I exercise. Thank you for your help with this. And so it is."

As you say these prayers, pay attention to any signs or guidance that you may receive, as well as ideas that may suddenly spring up in your mind. Sometimes, the changes will happen right away, sometimes it will be a more gradual process where you need to take proactive action steps too. Make a diary and write your angel prayers and results there. That way you will notice any recurring patterns that may emerge and gauge the progress you have made, as well as keeping you motivated throughout.

You can even write a letter to the angels, honestly expressing all your frustration and pent up feelings about your weight issue, before burning it or throwing it away. That will bring you a lot of relief. Do not censor yourself during this exercise, but aim to express your authentic feelings. Once that tension is out of the way, the solution and resulting action steps will be clearer for you.

Nature

The nature angels are Earth Spirits who rule over the flowers, plants, trees, soil, sand, rocks, stones and crystals; every living thing upon the planet. Nature angels live amongst plants and animals, and are responsible for the calming and healing effects that come from nature and the outdoors. Every living creature and natural elements, including the water and rocks, has guardian angels of different kinds. There are many different types of nature angels, including those considered to be mythical creatures: leprechauns, elves, fairies, brownies and tree-people.

The nature angels (also known as Elementals) are here to help create abundance and balance on the Earth, and are therefore always to be respected, appreciated, and honoured. They teach us how to nourish ourselves and live in abundance as co-creators in a space of balance and harmony. This means living responsibly and mindfully with regard to all life upon the planet. Stability and abundance can be manifested into every area of our lives when we focus on the powerful energy that flows around us in every moment.

Fairies can be found wherever there are plants and animals. They can sometimes be seen as tiny coloured lights or swirling mists. Fairies are primarily involved with healing humans, but also act as guardian angels for people whose life purpose involves conservation and animal welfare. Fairies also help us to release negative energies and thoughts that we may have absorbed by our own means through worrying, and from the influence of others in our lives. If you are out walking in nature, ask the fairies to surround you with their love, light and healing energies. Nature spirits help us to understand the natural rhythms of nature and to get a better understanding of our place in the world.

Tree and plant spirits also have great power to heal all our stresses and problems if we choose to work in unison with them. Find a tree that you resonate with, one that you really love, and ask to work with its spirit essence. Every species of animal has its own guardian angel too, so when you with your pet you are also interacting with your pet's angels.

There are also water spirits which rule over the water and tend to the creatures that inhabit this realm. These water spirits are here to teach us to cleanse and balance our emotions, and to go with the natural flow of things by taking the path of least resistance.

Nature angels also encompass fire spirits, often seen as Salamanders, which guard the secrets of the transformational energy of fire. Salamanders are often found around volcanoes in large numbers. Fire spirits teach us about the spark of our life energy which resides in all of us. This life-force that is within us all drives us forward and helps us to spiritually awaken. Fire purifies through burning, cleansing and destroying the old, and in doing so allows the new to emerge.

The spirits of the air are known as sylphs, and they work to carry our prayers and affirmations to the angels and the higher realms. Air is an element which is light, free and flexible. It is invisible and cannot be seen other than by its effect of the things it touches. Most life forms on Earth need air to exist and live. Sylphs encourage and increase our mental prowess and intuitive abilities, creative imagination, communication and inspiration. Creatures of the air such as birds and butterflies gladden our hearts, as well as bringing us subtle messages.

The easiest way to work with the nature angels is within the natural environment, whether this be a garden, park or beach. Here's one way that you can go about it:

- Take a moment to breathe in the fresh air and ground yourself. This is done by imagining roots growing out of the soles of your feet. These roots push themselves down into the ground, going deeper and deeper through the soil and rock below. They come to the centre of the Earth, where they find an enormous boulder. Anchoring themselves tightly to this almighty rock, the energy of the earth is sent back up through the roots, grounding you strongly.

- Stand near a tree or plant that you feel drawn to. Look at it with love and gratitude and intend to connect with the angels around it.

- Call out to the Nature Angels and request them to connect with you. You could say, *"Dear Nature Angels, I wish to connect with you. Please come to me now. Thank you."*

- You will intuitively sense the connection when it happens. You may sense a warm or loving energy in your vicinity. You may feel a tingling sensation within your body, or even feel soft brushes against your skin.

- Take a walk around the natural environment you are in. As you walk, request the nature angels to work on you and to clear you of all lower energies. Request them to help you raise your vibration.

- If there is anything bothering you, hand over your concern to them and request them to bring you clarity and healing.

- Spend at least ten minutes walking around, lying on the grass, leaning against a tree or just sitting quietly near a tree or plant. You can of course stay longer if you feel like. The Angels will be by your side and working on you all along.

- Once done, thank the Angels for their help.

Parking spaces

This is a request that needs to be seen to be believed but which has worked for me countless times: angels can get you parking spaces! When you set off on a journey, whether you are the driver or not, ask your angels for a parking space before you get to your destination by saying;

"Angels, I call upon you now. Please help me to get a parking space when I get to my destination. Thank you for this and all you do, and so it is!"

Visualise yourself driving into the space that you have asked for, and then sit back, relax and enjoy the journey. Low and behold when you arrive there will be the most perfect space waiting for you. A little thank you as you are parking the car and it is all done. You'll never be stuck for a space again! It may sound crazy, but just give it a try; you'll be amazed by the results.

Finding like-minded people

You may have picked up this book simply out of a curiosity or interest about angels, but there may be something far more meaningful going on. Throughout the modern world there are two types of very special people who are here to help others and the planet, and you may have picked up this book because you are endlessly searching for others who are just like you so that you don't feel alone and overwhelmed by the task at hand. These two types of people are Light Workers and Earth Angels, and let me start by explaining these terms for those who may be unfamiliar with them.

Before some people were born and came into being, they made a commitment in their spiritual selves to help the planet and the people upon it to heal from the effects of fear. These people are known as Light Workers. Each Light Worker is here for a very specific and divine purpose. However, many Light Workers forget their origins and soul contracts quite quickly after incarnating upon the Earth, due to the pressures and societal ideologies they are exposed to. A form of spiritual amnesia engulfs the mind, and these precious souls forget their divine and perfect identities. Not only this, but they also forget their abilities to miraculously help the earth and all living creatures. When Light Workers forget who they are and why they are here, they feel lost and afraid.

How do you know if you are a Light Worker? If you are, you will hold these attributes:

1. Feel a calling you can't ignore to heal others.

2. Want to help resolve and heal all the world's social and environmental problems.

3. Hold an unshakeable belief that spiritual methods can heal any situation.

4. Experiencing paranormal or spiritual phenomena, such as psychic premonitions or angelic encounters.

5. Been through some very difficult and challenging life experiences that have taken your thoughts away from your divine origins.

6. Understand that to heal the world you need to heal yourself first.

7. Feel compelled to share your healing experiences through writing, teaching, or counselling.

8. Have felt an unexplainable sense of time urgency to fulfil your scared mission without even knowing that you are here for a higher purpose. You may also be unsure what it is or how to fulfil it.

The other type of spiritual person on the planet is an Earth Angel. Do you feel different from other people, as if you were dropped off on this planet and wonder when someone's coming to take you home? If you have a passion and talent for healing, teaching, or helping others, yet you yourself have substance-abuse problems, weight issues, relationships challenges, and the like, then you may be an Earth Angel. Earth Angel are also highly sensitive and dislike violence in all of its forms.   If you're an Earth Angel, then you're a powerful Light Worker with a legacy of healing and miracles behind you in past lives, and in front of you. You have accepted your Divine assignment to come to Earth whilst in the higher realms and spread your teachings and healing energies to all. The characteristics of an Earth Angel are:

★ Feeling alienated, separated or different to those around you. You may have even been teased or bullied for the supposed different behaviour and interests others see in you.

★ Hyper sensitivity to chemicals, people and violence. Earth Angels have difficulty being around lots of people, as they will end up feeling bombarded by the overwhelming emotions and physical sensations that come from other people. Many Earth Angels have learned to avoid harsh chemicals in their food, cleaning supplies, and toiletries due to severe unwanted reactions. Violence in any form frightens and displeases Earth Angels, including arguments, negative media reports, and violent movies. They are often teased by others for this trait, who will say "You're too sensitive!" However, this sensitivity is a divine gift that Earth Angels bring with them to this planet, and they use it to intuitively know where their abilities and skills are needed. They couldn't turn off their sensitivity if they tried or wanted to.

★ A sense of purpose to their life that they can't ignore. Even if they don't know exactly what this purpose is, they feel instinctively drawn to helping and healing others.

★ Many painful and dysfunctional relationships. A lot of Earth Angels have parents and families who are emotionally cold or abusive. They may feel as though they don't fit in at all with the people around them, to the point that they may even feel adopted. The truth is that although these people are their physical family, they are not their spiritual family.

Instead, they have been sent to a family like this deliberately so that they can help to heal the various different members, but also to fast track their own spiritual growth and development. Earth Angels may also find themselves experiencing unbalanced friendships and romantic relationships, where they end up being taken advantage of, abused and generally mistreated. The only way to break the cycle of these kind of relationships is to understand why they keep ending up with people in their lives who treat them badly, and a commitment to change it.

★ Looking younger than their physical age. Whether it's their spiritual origins, or the fact that many Earth Angels truly look after themselves, there is usually a surprise when others find out how old they actually are.

★ Having a history of substance abuse and addictions. Whether it's turning to food, drugs, alcohol, cigarettes, relationships, or all of the above, some Earth Angels turn to outside substances or influences to numb the pain of feeling different in their lives, as well as being intimidated by their life's mission.

If you recognise yourself as either a Light Worker or an Earth Angel, or even if you have spiritual interests, you may find that you have gnawing sense of isolation, separation and being misunderstood by those around you. You may feel as though you are the only person on Earth like you, or even that you are some kind of freak or misfit. But nothing could be further from the truth. There are literally millions of people around the world like you, and the angels can help you to reach out to some of them so that you can have friendship, support and encouragement on your journey. First of all, as with everything you wish to manifest in your life, you need to ask the angels for help! Say,

"Angels, I call upon you now. I wish to meet and connect with likeminded people across the globe, whether they be spiritual, Earth Angels or Light Workers. Please help me to bring these people into my life so that I may enjoy the friendship and support on my life's path. Thank you for your help with this, and so it is!"

Once you have voiced your prayer, be open to the guidance that comes to you. You may feel drawn to pick up certain magazines or books, attend certain meetings, or join forums and groups dotted across the internet. Take the action steps you are guided to take and enjoy the connections that you make along the way. These people will truly make your spiritual journey easier and more enjoyable.

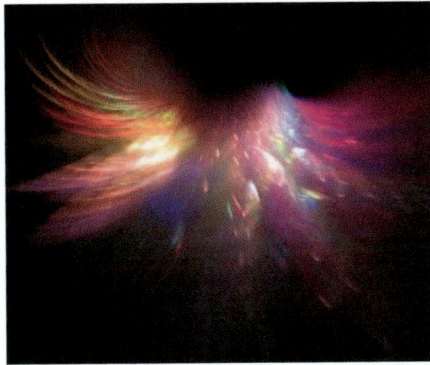

As you can see, the angels have limitless areas and problems they can help us with! Don't just limit yourself to this list however, feel free to call upon them for ANYTHING you need help or guidance with; no problem is too big or too small. Never feel silly for doing this or that you are wasting the angel's time. Remember that they are here to help us all be happier and more at peace, and they will do anything they can to help with this. It may feel uncomfortable or strange initially, but what have you got to lose? The worst that can happen is that your prayer or request goes unanswered, but just think about what benefits you could receive! Ask and be open and trusting to the guidance that you will receive, and the outcome can only be positive for you. Faith is everything when working with the angels, but the more you see them helping you, the greater your sense of trust and faith will be; believing is seeing.

The next chapter will look at other beings within the higher realms who are all ready and willing to help and guide you.

Chapter Ten

Ascended Masters

If you only connected with the angels and archangels for the rest of your life, you would still have a life that is full of blessings and miracles. But there are other higher beings who are available to you, all willing to work with you should you choose to call upon them. Although not necessary, think of it as having a full spiritual team behind you. When you connect and work with, not only the angelic realm, but the ascended masters as well you are establishing a strong group of higher beings whom you can call upon whenever you're in need of help or guidance.

Ascended masters are our elder brothers and sisters, in a spiritual sense. Most have walked the earth in past or recent ages, and through good works and devotion to their faith have balanced their karma, fulfilled their spiritual mission, earned their ascension into the higher realms, and no longer have to reincarnate. There are many available to you whom you can call upon whenever you feel in need. I am listing the most well-known ones, as well as a few whom I have connected with personally. If you wish to explore others, the book Archangels & Ascended Masters by Doreen Virtue (Hay House, 2004) is an essential text that details numerous higher beings for you to work with. At the end of the chapter I will give you a meditation exercise which you can use to connect to the ascended master or masters of your choosing.

Jesus

The most well-known of all of the ascended masters is Jesus, and we all have knowledge of him no matter what our spiritual background. Thought of as the world's greatest teacher, He holds love and devotion for the whole of humanity. Jesus reminds us to live in peace, brotherhood and to be of service to one another. For it is through our connections with each other that we can learn that we are part of a great worldwide community to which we all belong. Personally, I was highly resistant to connecting and working with Him at first. For me, his links to the Christian faith are so strong that I almost felt as though I was lining my own beliefs with the religion if I did work with him. And yet, like all ascended masters, Jesus will work with all people from all creeds and faiths if He is called upon. His divine qualities are to spread love, illumination and healing to every person who walks the Earth, and this means that His focus is not upon which faith you choose to practice.

Connecting and working with Jesus is an extremely powerful moment for everyone that calls upon Him. His light is so pure that it draws your eyes and heart, yet is almost too blinding to look at. The love that emanates from Him is unlike anything that you will ever experience upon the Earth. It is unconditional, pure and everlasting; the true love of God for each and every one of His children. Connecting to Jesus can bring you healing, help you to love all of humanity, and bring you great enlightenment away from strict dogma and rigid beliefs. Jesus works with the energies of Teaching, Unconditional Love, Forgiveness and Devotion to the Christ with-in. He also works to remove fears and feelings of self-doubt from us and to awaken the Christ Consciousness within us. His love for us and desire to see us become complete, perfect and whole is never ending.

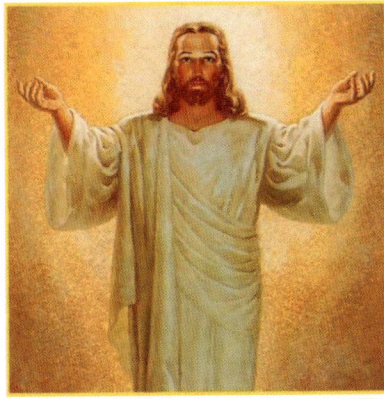

Mother Mary

Mary is the great representation of the Divine Mother, and has been revered greatly in the west for thousands of years. Her role as the virgin mother of Jesus has endeared to the heart of millions of people all over the globe, and many consider her to be the great spiritual mother. Ascended Master Mother Mary is here to work with the wounded mother in all of us – through all lives and dimensions, across all planes. Her love and her arms encompasses us all. Her work with the wounded mother in all of us includes men – as they too have been wounded mothers in past lives. Mother Mary, who volunteered before her birth to bring Jesus to the world. Also called "Mother of the World." A beautiful, powerful ascended master of great love, wisdom and compassion. She protects women and children and intercedes in healing.

Like Jesus, you don't have to be a believer of the Christian faith in order to connect with Mary; she is available to all those who wish to call upon her. She is wonderful for healing emotional problems, and working in tandem with Archangel Raphael (who works more on a physical level), can provide real holistic healing for all the issues you may be working through. Mary also brings her loving and nurturing essence to matters relating to families and children, so that all problems can be healed. She also helps us all to connect to the divine feminine within so that we can bring more balance to the patriarchal energy that has dominated the world for a long time. No matter why you call upon her, you can be rest assured that her energy is very loving and nurturing, and she will infuse this to help you solve any problem or issue that you need help with.

Ganesh

When facing challenges and obstacles on our path we can start to question the choices we have made and who we really are. Ascended Master Ganesh is the elephant headed Hindu God who will help you along your path, clearing obstacles and unexpected challenges. The key to removing obstacles is the willingness to move forward, to flow your energy with as much harmony and balance as possible, and Ganesh will certainly help you wish this. His energy is incredibly strong, and when you call on him you have to be prepared that he will bring up many things that you may not want to deal with but which help you move easier along your path. However, he is also very sweet and loving, so you don't need to worry that he will dominate you or connect with you in an aggressive way. Think of him as a tame elephant walking ahead of you and clearing all obstacles in your path.

Isis

Ascended Master Isis was the Egyptian goddess of Motherhood and fertility. She is here at this time to work with our crystalline bodies. As we ascend, more energy flows through our systems, Isis is here to help us cope with the changes. Changes not just on a physical level, but also emotionally and mentally. In Egyptian and Spiritual beliefs, Isis is associated with funeral rites, but as the enchantress who resurrected Osiris (after he was dismembered) and the mother of Horus, she is also a giver of life, a healer and protector of Kings. She was known as 'Mother of God' and is often represented with a throne on her head. Known as the Divine Mother, Isis is the goddess of wisdom and magic. She is working on the planet to help us to bring 'balance' into our lives, and is working with Saint Germaine and Master Serapis helping to clear any disharmony from conflict.

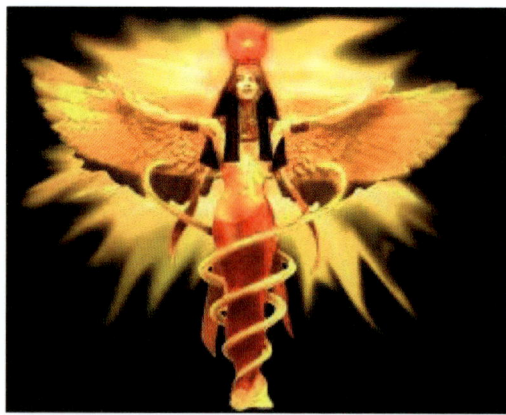

Lakshmi

In the Hindu tradition, Goddess Lakshmi is a bringer of physical wealth and abundance, also brings spiritual wealth, such as intelligence, enlightenment and the awakening to the God within. Lakshmi is described as being "as radiant as gold" and "illustrious like the moon." She is said to "shine like the sun" and "to be lustrous like fire."

But Lakshmi has a deeper, esoteric significance in that she is associated with immortality and the essence of life. She is often depicted with a lotus and an elephant. The lotus represents purity and spiritual power; the elephant, royal authority.

In her hand she holds a lotus flower. The flower represents the greatest treasure of all, the attainment of spiritual power and perfection through self-realization, or oneness with the Higher Self. Within the lotus flower, Lakshmi holds the key to the next stage of your spiritual development.

Kali

This Hindu goddess from India is known as the Goddess of Destruction or also the Endings and Beginnings. Although many fear Kali, she is a loving and peaceful energy that wants nothing more than to assist with the ending of cycles so as to harvest the new. She has intense and high energy as well as a very clear mission. She can be impatient and once you call on her for assistance, step out of her way and let her do what you have called on her to do. She instils courage, strengthens determination and focus, provides clear direction and motivation, and imparts protection. Also known as Black Mother, Kali-Ma and Raksha-Kal. Kali is the goddess of the ending of cycles, the death and transformation energy that lets go of the old and brings in the new. Kali is a loving energy that helps free us of fear, she only destroys that which keeps us in bondage, or which could slow or divert or divine mission.

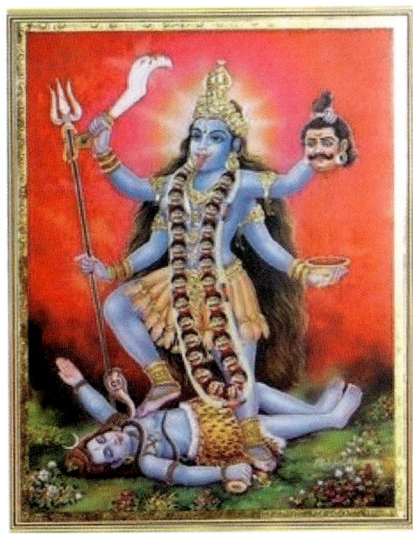

Mary Magdalene

Mary Magdalene, known also as Mary of Magdala is most widely known with Jesus, she was one of the closest to him, even staying with him even to the Crucifixion. She was the first person to whom Jesus appeared after his resurrection and the first to preach the "Good News" of that miracle. From other texts of the early Christian era, it seems that her status as an "apostle," in the years after Jesus' death rivalled even that of Peter.

Mary Magdalene is especially working with equal rights for both women and men through the spiritual, physical and mind. She brings self-confidence, strength, a deep feeling of self and re-assurance, opening new doors into your life and showing you a clear path with deep peace and re-assurance through her guidance. For those connecting with Mary Magdalene she comes forth very peaceful and is like your best friend, supporting you in every way. She is always willing to help anytime you need her.

Ascended Master Mary Magdalene works with the energies of the Divine Feminine. She stands with those who need warrior energy to deal with issues in their environment. Her life with Jesus was not her last life – but it is the life which has affected her for the last 2000 years. From the life they shared, Jesus became loved and revered by Christians for 2000 years – that loving positive energy going continually to him. Mary Magdalene received the opposite energy. She has been reviled and set up as an example of what a woman shouldn't be. In effect –she has had 2000 years of psychic attack. Imagine the lives she has had since then and having to cope with negativity coming to her from a world of Christians.

Mary Magdalene was Sarah, the wife of Abraham in a previous life. Abraham was a previous life of the Ascended Master El Morya. So Mary Magdalene has been both a revered and despised woman of Christianity. She truly is a warrior woman - she coped and through her adversity learned to love all of humanity, and so ascend.

She is a Master who is strong, yet gentle. There is humour and laughter – yet show her injustice and she stands ready to give her support. If there is an external battle – bullying, abuse, any type of external attack and she will help when asked.

Melchizedek

Melchizedek means 'King of Righteousness', and he lived on earth, but never lived or died. He serves with great love, power and authority, and is considered an equal to Archangels Michael and Metatron. Melchizedek is an ancient cosmic being in charge of the order of Melchizedek, which includes all who serve from divine guidance. This brotherhood organizes the Mystery School, which holds the secrets of God, the Universe and the true history of the planet, and is working to establish heaven on Earth. Jesus was a high priest in the Order of Melchizedek. All humans belong at some level to this order. Though he has lived on earth, he was not born and did not die. Melchizedek gifts mankind with freedom, forgiveness, and creativity, the science of alchemy and transmutation, and sacred ritual. Melchizedek was a Canaanite priest-king and teacher of the patriarch Abraham. He's associated with Archangel Michael and Jesus in many ancient spiritual texts… Melchizedek is reputed to be Noah's descendant and a great spiritual master of alchemy and sacred geometry. Call upon Melchizedek for help in mastering manifestation and to understand esoteric wisdom.

Buddha

Gautama (the Buddha who is devoting himself to being an ascended master) attained the enlightenment of the Buddha in his final incarnation as Siddhartha Gautama. He was born in northern India, about 563 B.C., the son of King Suddhdana and Queen Mahamaya. Soon after his birth, his mother passed on and he was raised by her sister. At sixteen, Prince Siddhartha got married and had a son. The turning point of his life did not occur until the age of twenty-nine, when he set out on four journeys, which presented the four passing sights: (1) a very old man leaning on a staff; (2) a pitiful man racked with disease lying in the road; (3) a corpse; and (4) a yellow-robed monk with a shaved head and a begging bowl.

Moved with the compassion by the first three sights, he realized that life was subject to old age, disease and death. The fourth sight signified to him the possibility of overcoming these conditions and inspired him to leave the world he knew to find a solution for suffering. He left his palace and wandered and meditated for several years and realized the Four Noble Truths, the Eightfold Path and the Middle Way. His philosophy, sometimes called the "Middle Way" formed the basis of Buddhism based on the eightfold way of right views; right intention; right speech; right action; right livelihood; right effort; right mindfulness, and right concentration. The energies of the Buddha are based around balance in all things; simplicity; inner peace through meditation and spiritual work on the Self; joy found in everything and loving acceptance of all living things. He passes during the full moon of May, about 483 B.C.

Gautama Buddha today holds the office of Lord of the World. At inner levels, he sustains the threefold flame of life, the divine spark, for all children of God on earth.

Connection to the Ascended Masters

Meditation with focused intention is the key to connecting with the ascended masters. Although they are available to call upon whenever you need help or guidance, just like the angels, by engaging in this kind of spiritual practice you can achieve more direct contact and even be able to communicate with them! There are two methods of ascended master meditation, although they both centre on the same practices. One is to determine which ascended master you wish to connect with before you meditate, so that you are in affect visiting their house when you open up your conscious mind. You can determine which one you wish to connect with by reading their specialities and focuses and linking in with your own current challenges. The second option is to meditate without choosing a specific ascended master before you start. Although you may feel this option may not bring you the guidance you are in need of, the higher realms know exactly what help you are in need of as they know the stresses and problems you are going through. Choosing this method of ascended master meditation means that you have complete faith in the angelic and higher realms to provide exactly the right help at the right time for you. Plus, it's always exciting to see who turns up for you! Once you have determined which method you wish to engage with, prepare yourself for the meditation.

★ Choose a time of the day where you can spare yourself at least 20 minutes. Choose a place where you won't be disturbed, and turn off all electrical appliances, including your mobile phone. If there are others around, let them know what you're doing and not to bother you unless there's an emergency.

★ Ensure that the room is of a comfortable temperature for you; you don't want it too hot or too cold as both are distracting. Adjust any clothing needs or air conditioning as appropriate

★ Sit on the floor or on a hard backed chair. Make sure your back is straight and you are comfortable (but not so much that you risk falling asleep!)

★ Close your eyes and draw your attention to your breath. Breathe in deeply all the way down into your stomach, and feel all the tensions and stresses leaving your body as you exhale. If there is any area of tension in your body, consciously look to relax it. This is done by tensing said area, then visualising all the aches and anxiety melting away as your relax.

★ Imagine yourself in a bubble of golden light that stretches from your feet all the way up to the top of your head. This bubble of light will keep you safe during the meditation, as well as helping to raise your vibrations in preparation for connecting to the ascended masters. Breathe in, and as you do so, see this golden light pouring into your body. See it lighting you up inside, filling every cell of your being, as well as the spaces between the cells. Imagine this golden Divine light filling your body entirely, so it shoots out the tips of your hair, your fingertips and your toes. You are completely filled with the light from the higher realms now and you are ready to connect with the beings that live there.

★ Now imagine your spirit leaving your physical body and floating up towards the ceiling. Trust that you are completely safe whilst this is happening, and that your body is being watched over by a multitude of angels. See yourself rising up through the roof of your house, up into the sky. Higher and higher your rise up, until you are floating through space and up to the angelic realms. As you arrive, you land at the foot of a small hill, adorned with a thousand beautiful flowers. The heady aroma of the blooms fills your lungs and you feel at peace.

★ Walk of float up the hill, and at the top you find a wooden bench. Sit upon it and either ask your chosen ascended master to appear to you within five seconds, or wait five seconds and see who does appear to you. If no one comes, ask the angels to strengthen your spiritual connection and ask again for an ascended master to appear to you. (Note: if still no one comes, do not worry. It's highly likely that it's not the right time for you to do this meditation. Perhaps you have been unwell, overly stressed or not been sleeping. All these things can block your connection, but it's not a permanent thing. Move to the end of the meditation where you return back to your body, and leave this until a later time when you feel more able to achieve the connection you are seeking.)

★ Once you have someone sitting with you, take in their appearance. What do they look like? Do they have any distinguishing features? If you are unsure of you are connecting with, ask the masters name. You can check this even if you are fairly sure of who you have with you, just to clarify things.

★ Ask them if they wish to do nay healing work on you first, or if they want to talk to you. If you feel they would like to heal you, allow this to happen. Let them do whatever they need to and enjoy the beautiful healing and loving energies that come to you. Once this has finished, or if they just want to talk to you, you may proceed.

★ Ask them if they have any opening words they would like to say to you. Pause and listen to their reply.

★ Ask them what they would like you to know and do about your current situations. Pause and listen to their reply.

★ Ask if they would like to connect with you again and when

★ Ask if there is anything you can do to strengthen your connections to the higher realms

★ Ask if they have any parting words for you, or if they would like to give you anything. If they do give you a gift, ask what the significance of this gift is and what you are supposed to do with it.

★ Thank them for connecting with you. You might want to hug them or bow. See them walk away or vanish before your eyes.

★ Walk or float back down to the bottom of the hill, before you begin your ascension back down to Earth. See yourself leaving the angelic realms, floating down through space. Enter the Earth's atmosphere and see yourself coming down through the sky. You enter your house and return back to your physical body.

★ Bring your focus back to the room you are in. With your eyes still closed, wriggle your fingers and toes, move your head gently side to side, and be aware of the temperature of the room. When you feel ready, open your eyes.

★ Have a pen and paper ready to jot down everything you can remember about the meditation: who you connected with, what they said, what gifts they gave you and if they gave you any healing. Feel the wonderful energies that they have infused into your body, and consider how you are feeling now. Happy, peaceful, relaxed? If you are feeling a bit lightheaded or spacey, drink some water to help ground you.

You can do this meditation as many times as you like to connect to all the ascended masters you wish to. Leave it to one ascended master per day though, as they are deeply powerful experiences that may prove to be too powerful if you engage with many of them. Take all the guidance, love, and support the ascended masters wish to give to you, and know that you have a strong spiritual team with you at all times.

Now you have experienced connecting with various beings from the higher realms, we will now look at how you can deepen this connection so that you engage with more advanced work and bring more blessings into your life.

Chapter Eleven

Developing Your Connection

By now you should hopefully be relishing having the angels in your daily life, as well as seeing their divine magic sprinkled over every inch. You may be happy to stop developing and learning at this point, and there's nothing wrong with that. For some, just establishing that angelic connection and noticing their presence is enough for them, and certainly if this you know that you have to do what is right for you. The aim of this book is to introduce as many people as I'm able to the angels, their love and guidance, so that you may enrich your life with their blessings. If you have achieved this then you can rest easy, but there are some who will crave more. These people want deeper connections with the angelic realm, and want to develop their spiritual work to take them to places completely outside of the known five senses. These last two chapters are just for you. If you do wish to stop before this point you can always look to develop the connection at a later date if you wish, once you feel more comfortable to do so. Spirituality is a very subjective and personal matter, and you always have to do what is right for you.

As mentioned, developing your angelic connection will take you to places that lie outside of the things that you can see, hear, touch, taste and smell on the Earthly plain. To truly deepen the connection you have built up, you need to step into the higher realms yourself. I will guide you every step of the way so do not feel anxious or worried about this. The angels too will continue to support and guide you with their love. I have said before that the angels are here to help us all be at peace and be happy, though ultimately they are also here to help us ascend through our spiritual journey to become enlightened beings. When you commit to increasing and developing your spiritual self, you can rest easy knowing the angels will certainly help you to do so; nothing will make them happier!

The first thing the angels can help you with is to promote your own spiritual growth. This is an essential starting point for all those who wish to deepen their connection, for you will connect easier and with more clarity when you have a higher vibration through spiritual growth. You will become more connected with your authentic self, as well as with the world around you. The result of this 'connectedness' is greater harmony and joy. Most of our lives are spent feeling separate and alone – and spiritual growth is all about returning to the feeling of one-ness that is our innate nature.

How does spiritual growth happen?

1. Read spiritual and uplifting books. Think about what you read, and find out how you can use the information in your life.

2. Meditate for at least 15 minutes every day. Introspection and self-reflection is essential for spiritual growth. We all need guidance, either from a human spiritual teacher or from the higher realms. The experience of connecting with your angels will open you to the guidance you need. The experience of connecting with your Higher Self is an experience beyond words – beautiful, emotional, safe, and loving.

3. Learn to make your mind quiet through concentration exercises and meditation.

4. Acknowledge the fact that you are a spiritual being having a human experience, not a physical body with a spirit. If you can really accept this idea, it will change your attitude towards many things in your life.

5. Look often into yourself and into your mind, and try to find out what is it that makes you feel conscious and alive. Feel your heart beat, the blood pumping through your veins. Listen to the chattering monkey mind that never ceases its incessant dialogue, and know that you are more than this. Discover your passions in life, what makes you jump for joy and smile from ear to ear. Live your life as though each day really were a gift, and be grateful for every blessing you have.

6. Consciously choose to think more positively. If you find yourself thinking negative thoughts, immediately switch to thinking more positively. Be in control of what enters your mind. Open the door for the positive and close it for the negative.

7. Develop the happiness habit, by always looking at the bright side of life and endeavouring to be happy. Happiness comes from within. Do not let your outer circumstances decide your happiness for you, for if you do this you can never be truly happy. Anything outside of yourself can be taken away from you, so basing your happiness around them will only lead to disappointment and upset. Learn to love who you are and to be truly happy inside. The longest relationship you will ever have is with

yourself, so make sure it's a relationship based around love and joy.

8. Exercise often your will power and decision making ability. This strengthens you and gives you control over your mind.

9. Thank the Universe for everything that you get.

10. Develop tolerance, patience, tact and consideration for others.

11. Surround yourself with people who are growing. Avoid or distance yourself from the energy vampires, the downers and the people who believe that there is no point in improving. The relationships you build as you expand your social circle are part of your increased connectedness with all life.

12. Find a balance. Take care of your body, mind and spirit. Don't undervalue and under-develop any aspect of yourself. Find a happy balance of exercise, nutrition, sleep, meditation/prayer, learning, creativity, exploring, etc. – don't neglect any part of yourself – these aspects of you give you a full life experience that you don't want to miss out on!

13. Recharge your spirit. That may mean time alone, doing whatever pleases you most; think of "me time" as a personal retreat that is as essential to your spiritual growth. You are meant to expand and to create – even if what you create is not a tangible thing, you are always creating the vibrational environment that brings – or repels – what you want.

14. Be of service. Service is what life is all about. When you develop your talents, you don't develop them for your own entertainment, right? You have a very deep desire to share the fruits of your talents – also known as service! In its essence, service is simply doing anything you can to improve the lives of others. A smile is service. A thank you is service. Anything you do with no thought of reward is service.

As you progress, you will naturally come to embody your spiritual growth and you will start to have the ability to allow things to happen rather than forcing them to. Going with the flow places you in line with the energy of the Universe. You may find yourself feeling so much more positive too! Not only will you radiate with an inner wellbeing, but you may even find yourself going about your daily life with a smile on your face! Developing spiritually means you know you're not alone in the world, that everything happens for a reason, and you can see how blessed you are. Who wouldn't be happy feeling this way? You may also find yourself drawn to helping others, animals and the environment as you become more and more aware of the true oneness of all life. Your empathetic and compassionate emotions will increase, and your aware ness of the world around you is something that won't be able to be ignored.

Becoming more spiritually aware allows you to be truly mindful as well. You'll find yourself unconsciously wanting to live in the present moment, and won't be overly worried or concerned about the events of the past, nor what might happen in the future. Due to this fact, and knowing that you have a spiritual cheerleading team by your side in every moment, means that ultimately you will also be eliminate feelings of stress, worry and anxiety from your life too. The love you have within your heart will increase tenfold, for others and for yourself. The negativity that is present in all corners of the world will not have the same power over which it once did, and you will find yourself being less judgemental and more tolerant of other people and their behaviour. You know that the way that people behave does not make them bad people, and you will see the inner light of the spirit that shines within everyone.

Ultimately, you will be living a life that is line with your purpose. You will know now that anything you dream you can manifest into reality for yourself, as you become more and more aware of your divine spiritual power. You will take true responsibility for your own life, and fully comprehend that you are more than your body, career, behaviour, words, religion, race or sexual orientation. You are a divine being and you can make your life whatever you wish it to be! The hardest part is starting; after that, just relax, learn, grow and flow. There is no point at which you will have arrived; no finish line, no end. Enjoy the journey! Spiritual development is an adventure. Anyone and everyone can grow spiritually. Making the choice to welcome life, light and love into your life is the best decision you will ever make. It is the basis for a better and more harmonious life for everyone, a life free of tension, fear, and anxiety. It is not a means for escaping from responsibilities, behaving strangely and becoming an impractical person. It is a method of growing and becoming a stronger, happier and more responsible.

Ritual for promoting spiritual growth

Engaging with this ritual can be an effective tool in raising your consciousness so that you can increase your angelic connections. The most vital part of this is *intention*, as it is this that will provide the power you are looking for. Before you begin, find a quiet place to relax and be still. Let your thoughts pass through your mind like fluffy white clouds through a blue sky as you focus on your breathing. You will find that your mind quietens down after a few minutes. Through this ritual you will create an amulet for yourself that will generate an energy field around you to help raise your vibrations. You will be able to carry, wear or sleep with this amulet, and you will find that it both seals and protects your aura. You will need a white tea light and a moonstone for this ritual that has been fashioned into a necklace or ring. These are available to buy at reasonable prices on the internet.

Do this ritual ideally on a Monday, as you will be working with the energies of the Moon and this is the day that is dedicated to it. Choose a time of the month where the Moon is waxing (growing larger), as this is the time that is normally linked spells for growth. This is perfect for this as you are looking to grow in your spiritual abilities, as well as increasing the protection round you. Perform the ritual outdoors if you are able to, or by a window if you're indoors where you can see the Moon.

- ★ Light a tea light before you start the ritual
- ★ Call upon Archangel Gabriel to oversee the whole process, as well as empowering you from within
- ★ Hold the moonstone in your left hand. This is the hand that links to intuition and feminine energy.
- ★ Sit in a posture that you would use for meditation purposes. Ensure your back sis straight, and breathe slowly and gently. Feel all you stresses and anxieties melt away

★ Feel your self breathing in the energies of the Moon, and visualise your body filling up with this beautiful energy.

★ When you feel the time is right through your intuition, breath this celestial energy into the moonstone

★ Hold the moonstone to your heart chakra and say *"Archangel Gabriel, please infuse this sacred crystal with your magical energy. Empower this stone and let it increase my spiritual awareness and abilities."*

★ Move the moonstone to your third eye chakra and say *"Archangel Gabriel, please bless both this gem and myself with your love and protection. Thank you for your help with this and all that you do. And so it is."*

★ Carry, wear or sleep with the moonstone on a daily basis to enhance your spiritual growth.

Determining your life's purpose

Each and every one of us has our unique purpose for being here on Earth. By focusing on it and ensuring that we are working towards it we will ultimately be both happier and healthier. When your soul was in the spirit world before you were born you worked with the angels to determine what lessons you would focus on in this lifetime, as well as what your purpose on the planet would be, so that you could help others and lead a life that is emotionally rewarding for you. Working on this also ensures that you focusing on soul growth, and the angels will be with you every step of the way to achieve the goals you have set yourself. The most powerful energy in the universe is love, and that is the main reason behind everyone's life mission. Thus, we are all here to learn love, remember love and teach love to all. Each and every action, word and thought either moves us toward love or fear. When we choose the path of love we grow spiritually and can fully help others. So, when you really get down to the bones of your life purpose it all revolves around what your love path will look like. Will you be a teacher, healer, parent, artist, caregiver, or any other role where you can spread love to yourself and those around you?

When people are looking to find their life purpose what they are ultimately looking for is a fulfilling role that will also allow them to be financially secure. They want to be able to quit the current job that is making them miserable so they can follow their joy, but also be able to pay the bills. This can be guaranteed to you, but only if you pay attention to the Divine guidance that exists inside you and follow the messages it gives you. The key angel for working on life purpose is Archangel Michael; he knows what everyone life's purpose actually is. Working with him, by asking him to help you work on your soul's life purpose, ensures that you will be able makes your dreams come true.

Your life purpose will never be things that make you uncomfortable or upset, instead it will follow those interests and subjects that already make you so happy. Thus, it will be focused on topics that you would do just for the love of them, even if you wouldn't get paid for it. Your inner joy and your life purpose are one and the same. Your Angels remind you that you bring your purpose to what you do. It reversed logic to think that your purpose directs what you are meant to do and that you will find joy by choosing "the right" work or career. When the Angels are asked questions about purpose, such as, "Should I be a doctor or a writer?" they universally answer: *Be happy, be joyful, be your true Soul-Self as a being of unlimited Love and unconditional compassion. Let the light of your soul shine with its pure radiant joy."*

If you are unclear about what these may be, ask someone you trust to point it out for you. They will have seen the things that excite you and make you happy, and can thus lead you in the right direction for your life's purpose. Once you start to follow your purpose, you won't wake up in the morning dreading the day and it won't feel like work. Instead you will become excited and invigorated about your journey and all the wonderful things in store for you! Abundance will then naturally flow to you as your mind becomes so positive and full of love. It really is a win-win situation for the whole world, including you! If you ever feel that you have lost your true purpose in life, you have lost your clarity about your source of joy and temporarily lost your connection to source joy. You can call upon your Guardian Angels and the Angel Ariel (who is the Angel of Joy) to help you reconnect with joy.

Do a short daily meditation and ask your Angels to help you regain your connection with your Soul Gifts and to help you restore the pure joy that is your Soul's natural state of being. It is not far away and the inspirations and impressions your Angels bring you will guide you step by step back into a more joyful state of being. Your Angels are offering your daily guidance during your daily mediations as "stepping stones" that will lead you into a greater and greater experience of joy in your daily life. You will naturally evolve in your work and it will grow and expand in step with your growth of joy consciousness. Be willing to let your career evolve and advance by daily increasing your joy and making career moves when the stepping stones appear. The more joy you can bring to where you are right now, the faster the next stepping stone will appear!

The Akashic Records

The Akashic Records can be likened metaphorically to a universal library or a cosmic computer, where information is stored on every soul that lives within the universe. Every thought, word, emotion, planet, being, idea, soul, consciousness, personality, and action throughout all aspects of time and space is stored energetically within it. In actual fact though, the Akashic Records are far more complex, vast, and of a higher vibration that can be simply explained through Earthly 3D terms. The very records of each and every soul throughout the course of its journey through time, space, physical and non-physical reality are held within held within the very fabric of creation.

The Akashic Records are an experiential body of knowledge that contains the energetic signatures of the origin of souls, previous lifetimes, soul intentions and purposes, and future points of choice and possibility. With each and every choice, thought and action, the Akashic

Records change and are updated in each and every moment.

How are they updated? This is one of the main roles of the powerful being, Archangel Metatron. Archangel Metatron energetically encodes and records in the Akashic Record everything that happens throughout existence. Due to this close work with the records, Archangel Metatron can also help you to gain access to the records of your soul, and to that which will serve you on your journey now. Through accessing the Akashic Records of your soul, you can align with past skills and resources, heal present blockages tied to the past, and learn about and heal the future from the present. The Akashic Records are everywhere, they're around you right now, and by attuning your consciousness to them you can tune into the knowledge, wisdom, healing and truth held within.

There is a meditation which you can do to access the Akashic Records for yourself, with the help of Archangel Metatron:

- ★ Choose a quiet place to meditate in where you'll be comfortable and undisturbed. Close your eyes and start by taking deep breaths as you shift your focus within.
- ★ Visualise yourself surrounded by a bubble of Divine white light, and then call upon Archangel Metatron to help you access the Askasic Records for knowledge, wisdom, healing and spiritual truth.

★ Breathe in the white light around you, and let go of tensions and stress through your exhalations. As you inhale, breathe in love, positivity and strength

★ When you feel ready, ask Archangel Metatron to guide your journey into the Akashic Records. Imagine a column of white light in front of you. This column is directly from the Divine and is pure love. Enter the column and feel yourself lifting up. As you rise you feel yourself connecting to the Source of All That Is

★ Let your heart open to this Divine connection. Feel your mind expand, your heart become fully open, and the energy of love, light and joy wash over you as you lift up through the column of light.

★ Go up for as long as you intuitively feel guided to. When you are ready step into the sacred space before you. Know that you have arrived and you are now fully emerged in the Akashic Records

★ Allow yourself to simply be here for a while. Notice the knowledge encoded within the light that is all around you. Feel the vast and intricately connected records belonging to each and every soul. Notice how each soul is closely tied to another, how each individual choice ripples out far and wide and influencing all. Feel your connection to the records, the Universe, to everyone and everything.

★ Think of a situation in which you would like some insight. Know that Archangel Metatron is with you to help you access the information that will most help you.

★ Ask your question, and allow the answers to appear in whichever way is most appropriate for you. For example, you may be handed a book, a mental movie may flash up in front of you, or you may simply download the relevant information directly into your conscious. If you find yourself doubting the process, or you tuning into the chatter of the ego within your mind, ask Archangel Michael to help quieten your mind so you can focus on what you are doing. Open your heart, gaze into the information emerging before you and receive the download, images, feeling, inspiration, knowing of a course of action, or whatever is available for you now.

★ When you have finished receiving the information you need, or the scene starts to fade from view, thank Metatron for his help and return back to column of Divine white light. Step into it and feel yourself sinking back down to the present point in time and space where your physical body is.

★ Gently and lovingly bring your aware ness back to your physical body by wriggling your fingers and toes, slowly turning your head, and then opening your eyes. Drink some water if you feel spacey or light headed.

★ Write down your insights, impressions and feelings of what you received. You might not fully understand the symbols, images and knowledge at first, but ask archangel Metatron to help clarify it for you and it will soon come into focus.

The Higher Chakras (8-12)

Chapter seven saw me describe the seven main chakras of the body that most people are familiar with, however some chakra systems work with twelve chakras! Familiarity with the 12 chakra system adds depth, context, and appreciation for your understanding of how chakras work and how to best balance energies in your life. Although the idea of a twelve chakra system is relatively new, it can lead you to an advanced spiritual awakening once you become aware of their presence and start to clear and open them. Chakras 8 through to 12 are the energy centres of higher awareness, and they exist in the etheric body as opposed to the physical body. I will list what each of them are called, what benefits they can give you and how you can work with them:

★ Eighth Chakra: Soul Star Chakra

This is the chakra that is linked to enlightenment and ascension, and can be summed up by the phrase 'I transcend'. Working with it means letting go of the negative baggage from the ego, and letting Divine white light of spirit fill your life instead. Through this chakra we are able to connect to our higher selves and to develop our own spiritual abilities. Some people may find working with this chakra quite challenging as it asks you confront and deal with beliefs that have been holding you back in your life up to this point. But, once you are fully aware of this information about yourself, you can move past it to make the positive changes in your life you need to make to live a happier and more balanced life.

Also known as the 'seat of the soul', the eighth chakra is located above the head, just above the crown chakra. It is typically a hand width above the top of the head, although for some people this can be as much as up to two feet (60 centimetres). It is sometimes called the seat of the soul, as it is the point where spiritual energy, and Divine love, enters the body. Via the gateway, divine light and energy filters down into the crown chakra for distribution throughout the body. The eighth or soul star chakra meanings relate to infinite energy, spirituality, supreme Divine wisdom and spiritual compassion. The chakra colour for the soul star is white, and white light may be generated from this chakra: the clear, luminous light which brings spiritual cleansing and healing. The key functions are a connection to all, the soul realization and purpose, along with infinite energy. The spiritual lessons to be gained through working with this chakra are transcending Karma, instant manifestation, accessing Akashic Records, and spiritual awakening.

The first step to activating this chakra is doing any type of spiritual work: meditating, channelling, chanting, yoga postures, or breathing exercises; all of which will invoke the Soul. You can also do a Soul Invocation:

I am the Soul.

I am the Light Divine.

I am Love.

I am Will.

I am Fixed Design.

Speak these words aloud whilst focusing on the soul star chakra. After each line, pause and feel the chakra respond to the powerful energetic vibration of each statement. When "I am the Soul" is invoked by speaking with the intent of identification or oneness with the Soul, the following response is evoked: the Soul Star increases in size, brilliance and radiation and the central channel of the body becomes filled with rainbow fire. When "I am the Light Divine" is spoken, the following response is evoked: the Soul Star sends forth a stream of rainbow fire into the central channel of the body. When "I am Love" is spoken, the following response is evoked: a rose pink down pour of energy from the heart of the Soul Star floods the central channel of the body. When "I am Will" is spoken, the following response is evoked: a royal purple, brilliant clear red, a white and indigo blue downpour enters and fills the central channel of the body. When "I am Fixed Design" is spoken the 7 energy centres along the spine intensify. This last line means that you came into this life with a specific

Soul purpose. Once the Soul Invocation has been said, the Soul Star will obey thought and move within the physical, emotional, and mental bodies, and the aura. It will expand or contract or send out a beam of energy and radiate various colours of light without conscious direction by you.

★ Ninth Chakra: Spirit Chakra

This charka concerns the soul blueprint: that is the individual's total skills and abilities learned in all the life times. In the ninth chakra you will attain all the Christ energy that has been unavailable to you before. The ninth chakra will reveal all your true potential in the mental and physical realm as a healer, teacher, or creator. Here you find knowledge of your true soul. This chakra, when opened will allow you to link to the expanse realms of spirit. Here you will remember your direct connection with Source, and your ability to communicate with light beings, angels, guides, and star beings from around the galaxy.

When this chakra is activated, you willingly surrender to the flow of Spirit and allow the blessings of Divine will to flow   into   your   experience. The full extent of your souls gifts and abilities are also available for you to access, perfect, and draw upon, along with the realization of your expansive ability to create, empowered through your direct connection to Source.

★ Tenth Chakra: Universal Chakra

This chakra represents the universal aspects of being. All That Is, is contained within one universal flow, and this chakra is the access point to that infinite flow of creation. When this chakra is activated you feel in close alignment to the Universe and All That Is. The pathway is paved for you to connect with the Divine light beings in the universe and to complete the alignment of your Divine light body with your physical being.

This chakra activated allows for your Divine light body to be fully constructed, allowing unlimited access to travel within the higher realms of spirit. Divine healing, balance and full access to the Divinity of your soul are possible with the activation of your Universal chakra.

★ Eleventh Chakra: Galactic Chakra

Your galactic chakra, when activated allows for advanced spiritual skills, travel beyond the limits of time and space, teleportation, bi-location, and instant manifestation.

Here you are able to reach anywhere in the realms of Creation, communicate with the highest vibrational light beings, ascended masters, and the great brotherhood of light. Here you are able to bring healing, insight and growth from the highest realms into your present existence. Activating this chakra within yourself brings balance to humanity, Earth, and the higher realms of spirit.

★ Twelfth Charka: Divine Gateway Chakra

With your Divine Gateway chakra activated, your Divine essence is intact. This chakra centre is the Divine light portal allowing your complete connection to Divine Source, and offering an open doorway to explore other worlds and realms.

Here, full ascension, advanced spiritual skills, complete oneness with Divinity and full connection to the cosmos, other worlds, and beyond is realized.

Here you enter the Super Galactic Realms, access the Divine Mother, and the Womb of the entire Universe. Activating this chakra allow you to access the Goddess light, become one with the Mother, and become a star gate yourself enabling peace, balance, and ascension to enter into humanity through you.

All the rays of the Divine, and all the qualities of the Divine represented by the higher vibrational beings align with you here.

Activate this chakra, and allow all the blessings to then flow back down. Divine light pouring down through your higher chakras, in through your soul star and down your spinal column, through your Earth Star Chakra and directly connecting to the light at the core of the Earth before flowing up in an unending loop of Divine awakening, presence, growth and advancement once again.

★ Earth Star Chakra: This can be seen as chakra number 0.

As a physical being on Earth, you have a unique connection with the Ascending Earth, and to All That Is.

Your Earth Star Chakra is your personal link the Earth's life force, to the crystalline grid, and to the Divine light contained within the Earth.

Divine light frequency flows up from the core of the Earth, up through your Earth Star Chakra and up into your Root Chakra. From there, it flows up along your spine in a column of Divine White Light. It then continues up out your crown chakra at the top of your head, connecting you directly with the Divine. Light then pours down around your entire being, and flows in through your Soul Star Chakra, and down through the 7 chakras contained within your physical body.

The light then returns to the Core of the Earth, and once again it flows up through your Earth Star Chakra, in through your Root Chakra and up along your spinal column. It flows up and out of your crown at the top of your head into the light, into direct presence with the Divine and All That Is before pouring down upon you, in an unending, Divine, energetic cycle.

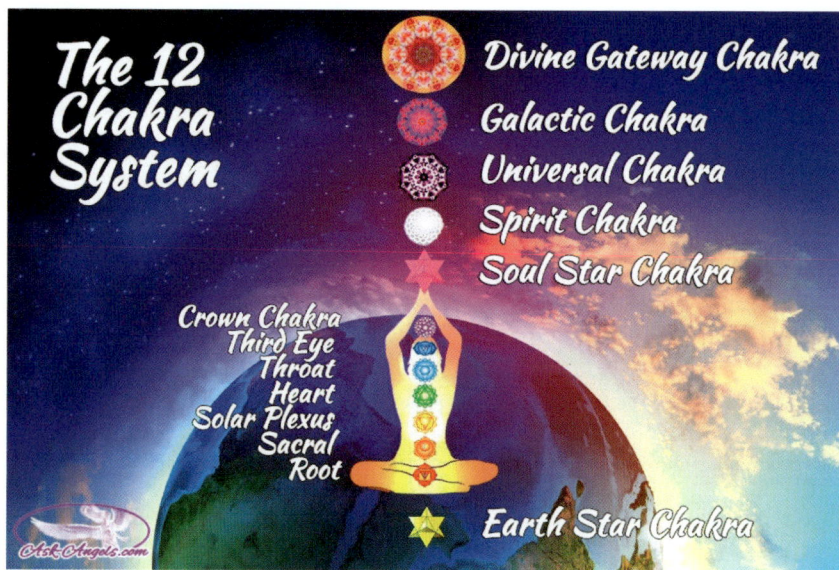

Metatrons' Cube

Metatron's Cube is a sacred geometrical symbol that forms a map of creation, and it is this 'map' that the mystics, sages and ancient civilizations have revered throughout the ages of time. Over 13 billion years ago, during what is referred to on Earth as the 'Big Bang', God gave birth to the Universe, and it is this symbol of Metatron's Cube that explains this 'birth' and the infinite expanding field of creation in all directions of time and space.

God's energy, through the field of Metatron's Cube, creates the potential field of creation – a field of high vibrational frequencies that ripple out through creation eventually creating colour, then sound and finally at their lower levels of vibration – physical matter.

Thus the field of God's energy (represented by Metatron's Cube) permeates through every level, through every aspect of creation. As that original spark of God's love moves in all directions of time and space- God is the energy waves, God is the colour, God is the sound and God is the physical matter.

God's light expands infinitely through Metatron's cube via one or more of the elements of creation – Earth, Fire, Air, Water coming together through Spirit. Galaxy's, solar systems, planets, humans, plants, animals, DNA, the atom, sub-atomic particles and hence the energy / space between all matter is made up of one or more of these elements.

Metatron's Cube is composed of 13 spheres held together by lines from the midpoint of each sphere. The spheres of Metatron's Cube represent the 'Feminine' whilst the straight lines represent the 'Masculine'. Thus Metatron's Cube represents the weaving together of the Male & Female polarities to create the oneness field of the infinite all.

13 Archangels of Creation

The 13 Spheres of Metatron's Cube are representative of the 13 Archangels that stand before 'God'. Each Archangel is a Sacred Keeper of an element of creation, and hence takes Gods love to expand the field of creation infinitely in all directions of time and space.

Thus the 13 Archangels (the 13 Spheres of Metatron's Cube) are present through all levels of creation from the highest vibrational frequency pulses at the central core of God/Source through to the densest of physical matter. Archangels are present everywhere, in each and every moment. Thus the Archangels are also present within you, they are you, and they create you.

As the Archangels are 'within you', for healing within our lives we have the potential to invoke an Archangel through us (through our 13 Energy Centres) in order bring balance to a particular Element or Elements and hence transcend disease and co-create health, vitality and well-being.

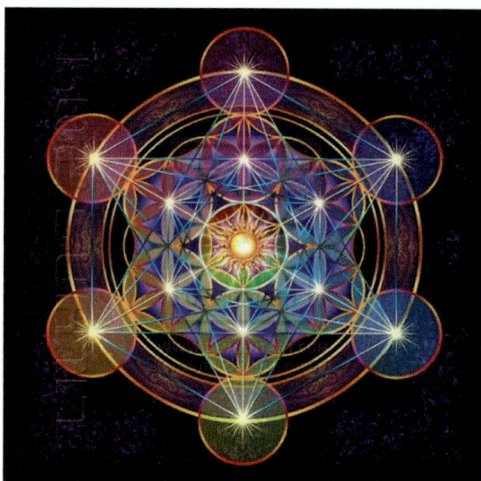

These are just a few ways that you can deepen your angelic connection, should you so wish to. The final chapter of the book concerns the greatest and most desired method of connecting with the angels: to actually communicate with them!

Chapter Twelve

Communicating with Angels

Much of what I have shared with you throughout this book relies heavily on your own sense of belief and faith. You have to trust that the angels are with you on a daily basis, and that they are helping you in every area of your life. There will be those who may be more cynical or sceptical about the whole thing- putting signs and miracles down to mere coincidence. However, what if you could actually communicate with the angels? Have a dialogue with them, where you talk and you hear their replies? This is the dream for so many people there, and this chapter will show you how to go about it!

The key method to really open up this dialogue between you and the angelic realms is meditation. Through purposeful and guided mediations, you will be able to meet, talk to the angels and get the guidance you need. Not only this, but the more you connect, the stronger your intuitive muscles will become. As this starts to happen, you will find that you do not necessarily need to enter a meditative state in order to converse with the angels. My own intuition and psychic abilities are so strong now that I can talk to the angels as I go about my daily business! But, more on that later. Fist, let me give you the guided meditations you will need in order to make the close connections that you are longing for.

Follow each of the guided meditations given below. You may feel more drawn to one over another, or you may wish to try them all and see which one works for you. Don't worry if one method doesn't seem as effective as another, this is a very personal journey and the whole thing is very subjective. You may wish to record yourself reading the steps given and then play them back when you're ready to meditate so that you have no distractions; again, do what works best for you.

As with all meditations given within the book, ensure that you find a comfortable and quiet place to do this where you know you won't be disturbed for at least half an hour. Turn off all technological devices, and inform your loved ones not to bother you whilst you are doing this. Make sure you have a hard backed chair to sit on, or you can sit on the floor and lean against the wall. Ensure you are warm enough, but not too hot. You may wish to have a glass of water to hand, as well as a notebook and pen to record the messages you receive within the meditations.

Start each of the three given meditations in exactly the same way:

★ Close your eyes and shift your focus to your breath. Take a deep breath in through your nose all the way down into your stomach. Hold this for a second and then exhale slowly. Do this at least three times. Continue to breathe deeply throughout the meditation, as it will help to relax you as well as helping to shift your own vibration to the higher angelic frequency.

★ Now imagine a ball of golden light all the way around you, from the tips of your toes to the top of your head. Breathe in and feel this golden light pouring into your body, lighting up all the different organs, muscles and even the cells of your being. Feel yourself filling up with this light until it's practically shining out of you.

★ Imagine a bubble of platinum light surrounding the room you are in. This will protect you from any lower or negative energies whilst you are in a meditative state.

★ Feel a beam of angelic light shining down on you from the Heavens. Notice the colour of this light, as it will be appropriate for the things you need at that moment (green for healing for example)

★ See this light grow bigger to shine directly over the town or city you are in, shining down on every being there. Grow it even wider then to encompass your whole country, before making it big enough to shine down on the whole world. Know that your light of love and healing is touching every single being upon the Earth.

★ When you're ready, bring the light back down to shining over your country, your town or city, your home, and finally you. Breathe deeply. You are now ready to begin your angelic connection.

1. **Meeting Temple**

★ Knowing that your physical body is safe and protected, visualise your spiritual self rising up out of your body towards the ceiling. Go right up through the roof of the building, and see yourself floating upwards in the sky. Higher and higher you go, right up into outer space. As you look down upon the Earth, you see a small portal next to you in the blackness of space. This is the gateway to the angelic realms, and you pass through it easily and safely.

★ Upon entering, you find yourself standing before a great temple. Notice what the temple looks like in style- Grecian perhaps, or maybe more Egyptian? Whatever the design, once you feel ready, you move forward and enter the doors.

★ In the centre of the space there is a chair waiting for you. This may be a simple wooden one, or a more elaborate affair with crystals and gems adorned upon it. Regardless, you know this chair is for you and you head over to sit upon it.

★ As you sit upon the chair, you are approached by an angel. Notice what they look like- appearance, clothing, gender, etc. If no name comes to you, ask them what their name is. The first name that comes to mind will be theirs, even if it is one you haven't heard of before or it makes no sense to you.

★ Ask the angel if they have any opening words they would like to say to you, then wait for their reply.

★ Ask the angel what is the main thing they would like to say to you at this moment? Wait for their reply.

★ Once they've finished, ask the angel if they would like to perform any healing on you. If so, allow this to happen as the angel deems fit. They may send energy beams to you, lay their hands on you, or any other array of techniques. Once the healing has completed, the angel will finish what they are doing.

★ Once this is done, or if the angel does not want to give you any healing, then ask them if they have any closing words they would like to say to you. Wait for their reply.

★ Ask the angel if they have anything they would like to give you. This could be a crystal, flower, animal, or anything they deem appropriate. Ask the angel what is the significance of the gift they have given you, and what you're supposed to do with it. Maybe you are supposed to place it in your heart, put it in your pocket, or allow it to travel alongside you. Whatever the answer, place the item where it is supposed to go.

★ Thank the angel for everything. You may want to embrace them if you feel so inclined.

★ Stand up from the chair and exit the temple, knowing that you can return here whenever you wish. Once outside, exit the portal from the angelic realms back into space; see the portal close behind you.

★ See you spirit slowly begin to descend back to Earth, through the sky, into the building you stated, and safely back into your physical body.

★ When you're ready, bring your awareness back to the room. Notice the temperature of the air around you, wriggle your toes and then open your eyes.

★ Drink the water and write down everything that happened during this meditation, so you can reflect back on it when you are ready/

2. <u>Direct Method</u>

★ Breathe in and as you do so, imagine yourself drawing in a beautiful golden and pink light into you being. Continue to breathe this in and imagine this light now raising your energetic vibration even higher. You may feel a tingling sensation in parts of your body, or a lovely warm glow spreading its way through you.

★ Mentally ask an angel to appear alongside you in the room within the next five seconds. As you count down you may sense them appear out of thin air, walk into the space, or even fly down!

★ Take a moment to get a sense of what this angel looks like. Are they coming to you with a male energy or a female one? What does their face look like? Their hair? What clothes are they wearing?

★ Ask the angel what their name is. Accept whatever name comes to into your mind, even if it is open you are completely unfamiliar with. You can ask the angel to spell the name for you if you are having trouble understanding it. You may also think the name you receive is too plain or 'normal' to be linked to an angelic being, but the angels can use any name that they choose, regardless of its origin.

★ Ask the angel if they any opening words which they would like to say to you. Listen for their reply.

★ Then ask the angel any questions or problems which have been taking away from your happiness. Whether its career, relationships, financial concerns, life purpose, or anything else that is causing you immense feelings of stress, the angel will be able to give you the guidance you are seeking. Remember that the angel's role is to help bring peace and happiness to each and every person on the planet. If you ask for their help in achieving this, they will do all they can to help bring these feelings to you. No problem is too big or too small; if it's causing you anxiety then talk to the angel about it.

★ Listen to what the angel has to say to you in relation to your problem. They may give you guidance, comfort or encouragement. Know that you can also ask for clarification or for them to expand on any detail if you need them to.

★ Ask the angel if they have any closing words which they wish to say to you, and listen to their reply.

★ Thank the angel for their help and guidance during this meditation. You may want to hug them if you feel drawn to.

★ Watch the angel leave the space or fade away from sight, then bring you awareness back to the room you're in. Wriggle your fingers and toes before slowly opening your eyes.

★ Drink some water and then write down everything you can recall about the mediation you have just experienced.

3. **Special Location**

★ Imagine yourself in a location that makes you feel peaceful and happy- whether it's a beach, forest, by a great lake- wherever you can feel safe and relaxed.

★ At this location of your choosing there is somewhere for you to sit- a log, bench, big flat stone- sit down upon it.

★ Take a moment to take in the scenery of where you, and feel your whole being growing very relaxed.

★ You notice an angel walking towards you. They sit down beside you.

★ Notice the angel's appearance and dress. Are they dressed in a particular colour? Do they have large prominent wings, smaller ones that are tucked away, or no wings at all?

★ Ask the angel's name and listen to their reply. Accept whatever comes into your mind, and ask them to repeat it if necessary.

★ Ask the angel if they anything they would like to initially say to you, and listen for their reply.

★ Ask the angel to show you what your life will look like in the next five years, and allow these images to come into your mind? Where are you living? Who are you living with? What does your house look like? What job are you doing? What are you doing in your spare time? Note all the details and ask the angel to clarify any details if you're unsure of anything.

★ How does this future make you feel? Surprised? Happy? Excited? Maybe you're worried about how things will change for you.

★ Ask the angel to give you guidance about how you can start to make your life become what you have just seen, and listen to the points they give you. They may give you a step by step plan for you to follow, or more general things that you can start to incorporate into your now. If you're still unsure or worried about anything, just ask the angel to give you more details and support.

★ Ask the angel if they have anything else they would like to say to you, and listen for their reply.

★ Thank the angel for their help and embrace them if you wish to do so.

★ Watch the angel walk away from you or fade from sight.

★ Bring your focus back to the room your physical body is in. Gently wiggle your fingers and toes before opening your eyes.

★ Write down everything that you saw and heard during the mediation to reflect upon, and drink some water.

Taking it further

I hope that you found these angelic mediations incredibly interesting and enlightening. Know that you can do them in any order you wish, and as many times as you wish to. By starting to purposefully connect with the angels through meditation in this way, you are inviting them even more into your life and making it known to them that you want to work with them more in every aspect of your life. The more meditations you do with the angelic realms, the higher your vibration will be and the more open you'll be all the time to their guidance and help.

Having worked closely with the angels for a long time now, I know that there comes a point where you don't actually need to be in a meditative state to communicate with the angels: you can actually connect to them whenever you like, wherever you are! How does this work? Let's say you are on a country walk. You may be on your own or with loved ones, but it's a beautiful day and the peaceful sounds of nature are making you feel relaxed and at peace with the world. Your mind naturally wanders to a situation in your life that is not how you wish it to be, and it's been causing you some stress. You find yourself talking to the angels about it in your mind- how you feel and why. You ask them to help you in giving you some guidance in making the situation better; giving them the permission they need to intervene. You start to notice that answers are coming to you within you mind, but how do you know this isn't just you making things up? Well;

- The words that are coming to you may not be things that you would naturally say in everyday day conversation
- The voice may sound different to yours in tone, pitch, or even gender!
- The words coming are all very loving, supportive and encouraging. They are *never* judgemental, angry or accusing.
- They will use words like 'you' and 'we', rather than 'I' and 'me'.

You listen to the guidance that comes through and take real note of it. So much so that, on returning back home, you start to act upon the guidance given to you, and you see really positive changes and miracles occur through this action. There's no doubt that you have received angelic help, and you haven't had to have been in any kind of meditation or trance to receive it! Not only this, but you can talk to then angels whenever you want to. Once you have given them permission to help you, you can trust that they will. By listening to the words that you receive and acting upon them, you can truly open the doors to communicating with the angels on a regular basis, and create miracles in your own life every day!

"We are with you every moment of every day. You are never alone or without support. We are not up in the sky or just some mythological beings; we are very real and right next to you this very moment. We are here to give each and every one of you the love, happiness and peace you deserve. Know that you are worthy of these things in your life, and we can help make them a reality, if you allow us to. Do not put off your happiness until tomorrow. Do not accept any more stress or upset in your life with a tearful shrug, as though you have to accept it as your lot in life. Life is not meant to be a struggle for you, dear one. Life doesn't have to be an uphill climb that nearly breaks you with every step. Life is a blessed miracle. Let us help you to see that. Let us shine love into your heart so your whole being shines brightly out to others. You are a miracle. You are a blessed child of God. And we are with you to lift to your highest and greatest good."

I hope this book has shone a light on the angelic realm for you, and you can see how inviting them into your life can really add a big sprinkling of magic to each and every day. I hope that each and every one of you brings a little angel love into your own life, as well as getting the help you need to live lives of peace and happiness. Angel blessings to you all.

Angels around us, angels beside us, angels within us.
Angels are watching over you when times are good or
stressed.
Their wings wrap gently around you,
Whispering you are loved and blessed.

- Blessing

24564526R00144

Printed in Poland
by Amazon Fulfillment
Poland Sp. z o.o., Wrocław